Jane

a memoir

by Jane Stanley

The Nautilus Publishing Company
426 South Lamar Blvd., Suite 16
Oxford, Mississippi 38655
Tel: 662-513-0159
www.nautiluspublishing.com

First Edition

Front cover design by Carroll Moore; front cover illustration by Emmitt Thames

Library of Congress Cataloging-in-Publication Data has been applied for.

Printed in the United States of America

10   9   8   7   6   5   4   3   2   1

To the five grandchildren who swim in my gene pool

PROPHECY

1

One fall morning in 1968, the air was crisp and blowy. I stretched out on the floor with the windows open to play with Harry, who was 18 months old. We lived on Southern Circle in Gulfport, Mississippi. Our yard backed up to the 18th hole of the Great Southern Golf Course. Harry enjoyed standing at the windows to wave at the passing golfers and neighborhood dogs. On the radio, Glen Campbell was singing, "Wichita Lineman."

My front door bell rang. I walked to the door and saw through the glass a rotund, short woman, in a multi-colored Muumuu. Her hair was pinned up in bright pink sponge rollers. She was singing to her Chihuahua.

I opened the door. The woman stopped singing and swaying.

"Can I help you?"

"No, child, I'm here to help you. But my dog, HuaHua — she pronounced it *WaaWaa* — is hungry. You got any hot dogs?"

"I'm sorry, do I know you?"

"No, but I know you. And I know your husband Neil White the Junior and it's him I come to talk about."

I couldn't imagine what this corpulent woman would know about my Porsche-driving, starched-white-shirt, neck-tie-wearing, lawyer husband. With trepidation, I invited her in. I picked up Harry and put him in the playpen. As soon as I put him down, he backed into the corner of the pen and stared.

She introduced herself as Pastoress Eula Jones, a tent revival evangelist. Then, she whirled her massive body around as graceful as a ballerina.

Holding HuaHua, she shouted *Shan de la cah, holin meh kin no foooooooooooaaaaah-hhhhh*. She continued to twirl shouting gibberish. I assumed she was speaking in tongues.

When she stopped, she reminded me her dog was hungry. I led her to the kitchen and pulled out a package of cold hot dogs. Before I could put them down on the table, she took the package out of my hand. I leaned down to get a sauce pan to boil some water. When I stood, Miss Eula had opened the package and was feeding her dog the cold hot dogs.

"I'm here to give you a prophecy," she said.

"A prophecy? About what?" I asked.

"It's about your husband," she said. "It came to me this morning from the very mouth of El Shaddai himself!" She looked down at the empty hot dog package. "Have you got any more of these?" she asked.

Anything to get rid of her, I thought.

I went to the cooler, pulled out a brand new bag of wieners. She took the whole bag, sat at my breakfast table, put HuaHua in her lap and the two of them started eating.

I didn't know what to say.

"Come sit a bit," she said, inviting me to sit at my own table. "You need to hear this so you can get yourself prepared." Miss Eula grabbed my hand and held it tight. "You listen good, Mrs. Jane White, because you are in for a ride. Your husband is going to have a spiritual conversion, just like ole Saul/Paul had. *Shan de la cah!*" She looked me directly in the eye and added, "He gonna see Je-Sus!"

I was stunned.

Miss Eula slapped the table and said, "Mr. Neil White, the Junior will leave this town, study for the ministry, and become a preacher man. A preacher man!"

I laughed out loud.

"Miss Eula, I don't think so. How do you know my husband anyway?"

"Well, there now is a story," she said, as she stood, walked into the den, and sat on the huge recliner. I followed her and sat on the edge of our brick fireplace.

Miss Eula got comfortable on the recliner, stroked HuaHua, and continued her story.

"I was holding a revival some 30 years ago and one of them fellows filled up with the Satan evil, commenced to shout me down while I was preaching. He just wouldn't quit. I picked up the first thing I saw — a Barq's Root Beer bottle, full to the top — and whacked that devil over the head til he shut his mouth."

Miss Eula paused as if she were reluctant to go on.

"I hurt him something awful. I was carted off to jail."

I glanced over to check on Harry in the play pen.

"Your husband's grandfather," she continued, "Mr. Walter H. White, Esquire, was my attorney and he come to get me out of jail. I couldn't pay his bill so he talked his son Mr. Neil White the Senior into letting me babysit your husband to work off the bill. I babysat him until he was four or five years old. He was some kind of mischief."

"Well," I asked, "why haven't I heard about you?"

"That's the thing," she said, "I moseyed on over Louisiana way for nigh on to twenty years or so saving some of them heathens and I come back several years ago. This is my home."

"And God spoke to you," I asked, "this morning?"

"*Shan de la cah!* Indeed, he did. Now I'm here to tell you don't you worry. When things go awry just keep your mouth shut and pray. Everything will work out just fine. God the Lord is good and He will see to it, Amen!"

I wanted this woman to leave.

"Miss Eula, I don't know what to say. But thanks for sharing your prophesy. I suppose I have some thinking to do."

"Yes, Ma'am, you sure do. I'll be in touch. You got any more hot dogs in that big freezer of yours?"

"No, you got them all."

"Well, that's a pity."

She hiked Huahua up, placed him on her large bosom, and walked out the door.

I plopped down on the couch and looked over at Harry. I wish I could have asked him if that really just happened.

• • •

When Neil came home after 18 holes of golf, I told him about Eula Jones.

"Yeah, I remember her," he said. "I think she's a nut case." Then Neil poured himself a drink and added, "I'm the last damn person God would have as a spokesperson."

I couldn't have agreed more.

THE
EARLY
YEARS

The James family in the Philippines (L to R: Viola James, Fred "Papa" James, Garner James, and my mother Elizabeth James.

2

In our household, a work ethic was second only to a Baptist doctrine. In the First Baptist Church of Gulfport, Mississippi, the membership was 100% white. The black janitor was the only man of color to ever enter those hallowed halls during the years of my youth. However, some of my extended family had experienced living and working with foreigners or people of color. After World War II, my mother's sisiter Aunt Viola had a job with the American Red Cross. Her posting was in Calcutta, India. She lived and worked with the native population, some darker in skin color than others. When my daddy found out about her going to India, he said, "Vi will rub elbows with those strange talking darkies and probably enjoy it, but not me," he said.

My maternal grandparents, Floy and Papa, had lived in the Philippine Islands from the turn of the century until the dawn of World War I. While living there, Floy and Papa had three children, my mother Elizabeth, my uncle Garner and my aunt Vi. They were accustomed to sharing life with people of different colors, cultures, and faiths.

To my daddy, our local people of color were "Nigs." Each time he said that word, either Mama or Floy scolded him and repeated that in the eyes of God all people are of equal importance. They believed the differences in individuals come from lack of opportunities, lack of access to information, and lack of care from narrow-minded people such as himself.

Daddy laughed and said, "I'm tired of lectures on my lackses."

My father's dad died when my Daddy was two years old. Daddy's

My father, Harry Stanley, as a boy in West Point, Mississippi

only role model was his grandfather Captain Abel Harrington. He had served in the War of 1860. Daddy called him "Cap'n Abe." They were all dirt poor. Daddy quit school in the sixth grade to go to work to support himself and his mom. At night he pedaled the player piano for the silent movies. During the day he dug ditches for the first gas lights in Columbus, Mississippi. Because he was a white boy, the supervisor made Daddy the team leader over nine huge black men. Daddy admitted it was those men who taught him how to labor hard with little monetary return. However, Daddy's grandfather, a Civil War veteran wasn't civil to blacks.

Daddy's heritage from Capt'n Abe was to work hard, care for your family, stand tall for what's right, and don't let the "niggers" get you down. Daddy inherited this nonviolent disregard for blacks just as surely as he inherited his coal black hair and blue eyes from his Anglo-Saxon ancestors.

When Daddy's mother developed breast cancer, they moved into a house across the street from MSCW ("the W") in Columbus. Daddy was promoted to a desk job. On weekends, he played the clarinet in a small band. The bands major gigs were playing for dances at Mississippi A and M College in Starkville and at MSCW.

The dances at the "W" were for women only. One night while Daddy was performing a solo, he spotted my mother waltzing with a tall, graceful blonde. He lost his place in the music, backed up, and tripped over a music stand, falling on his rear end. He always said her beauty literally knocked him over.

One Friday evening, they drove to Belfontaine, Mississippi to elope. The marriage, a violation of MSCW policy, caused my mother to be expelled. Daddy took a job with the Mississippi Power Company. He was transferred to Gulfport, where Mother's family was still living. When they moved to Gulfport Mother continued her education at Tulane and earned a degree in social work.

Daddy married a woman, my mother, whose father — my Papa —

My father, Harry Stanley, in 1934

My mother, Elizabeth James Stanley, in 1934

was a died-in-the-wool Yankee. He had no problem being courteous to blacks or to the hoboes who occasionally came to our door looking for handouts. Her mother, my grandmother Floy, was a saint. Floy taught me that "white folks were as good as blacks any day of the week." But more than anything else, Floy was kind. To everyone.

Even though we lived within 1,000 feet of the Negro community, and even though our neighbors had black maids and yard men, my family never employed house help. We did on occasion get Ole Sam to do a few yard jobs — more to justify giving him money and treating him with dignity than our needing help.

Floy was compassionate for folks regardless of their color, culture, or background. I found them intriguing. My first close contact with a black person was Sam. He tottered across the tracks and shuffled down our sidewalk supported by a knobby walking stick. One of our neighbors who was not a churchgoer kept a tin pan and mug hanging on her back stoop. When Sam begged at her door, she put leftovers in the tin pan and offered it to Sam. He had no fork or spoon so he used a rusty knife he kept in his pocket. He spilled a lot of food. My neighbor Joe told me his mama wrapped up food in a paper bag and gave it to Sam to eat under the cool of her pecan tree.

When Sam came to our back door, Mama waltzed through the kitchen singing:

> *The Beggar Brown is back in town*
> *Hungry for his fare*
> *Please nourish him, nourish him with care.*

Floy stopped her chores, took down a china plate, and fixed Sam a hot lunch. While it was cooking, she went to the back door to call, "Samuel Brown, good day to you!"

"Mornin', Ma'am," Sam replied.

"You may gather those hen eggs while your lunch is cooking," she said, handing him a basket.

"Mighty kind, "Ma'am," Sam said as he moved toward the chicken coop.

Floy generally asked Sam to gather hen eggs or to clip her favorite camellia bush. She told me, "It demeans a man to give him food without a dash of self-worth thrown in."

When Sam finished gathering eggs, Floy invited him to eat at the kitchen table.

On days when Sam would not come in the house to eat, Floy served him lunch on a tray. She sat down on the back steps beside him, tucked her skirts up under her knees, and preached to Sam about his soul, like the good Baptist she was.

Sam was so busy "Yes, Ma'aming" Floy he hardly had time to chew his food.

One day when he was eating on the back steps, he let my playmate, Cynthia Melvin, and me touch his mahogany skin. It was leathery and dry like the saddle Daddy kept in our garage. Sam's yellowed eyes watered most of the time and the tears ran into his white, prickly beard making it look like frost on a late October morning. His long, torn fingernails were caked with dirt. His clothes were stained and sweaty and he wore a hat, the brim limp and crumpled. Sam smelled like wood smoke and like he'd wet his pants.

One Saturday afternoon, Mama and Floy had gone to a ladies tea. My sister Harriet was off on her bike with Joe Melvin and Ed Fant. Daddy was napping.

I was hanging by my legs on the sack swing that was tied to a limb on the oak tree behind our house. I saw Sam walking up our driveway.

"Afternoon, missy," he said, "Your granmama home?"

"Nope," I answered, "She and Mama are gone."

"Your daddy home?"

"Yep. He's in the house."

"Go ask him if he get a bite of food for Ole Sam."

Obeying Sam, I skipped into the house and tiptoed up to Daddy.

He opened one eye. "What you want, Janie?"

"Ole Sam's outside and wants something to eat."

"Tell that damn nigger to get out of my yard. I've got no food for him today."

"But Daddy," I whispered, "he's hungry."

"He's not hungry. He just enjoys beggin'. Now get."

I didn't want to disobey Daddy, but I also didn't want to tell Sam to get out of the yard. I walked slowly to the back door. I stepped outside chewing on my bottom lip. I looked at Sam, shrugged my shoulders, and spread my hands in a gesture which said nothing. And everything.

"It's all right, Missy. I'll come sometime when your granmama be home."

Ole Sam walked back down the driveway and turned north toward the tracks.

3

I skipped to the swing, crossed my legs over the burlap sack, held on to the rope, and leaned far back. My head dangled in the air. I looked straight up and saw clouds sailing past. One was shaped like smoke coming out of a huge ship's funnel.

I remember Floy telling me she once had sailed on a steam ship all the way across the Pacific Ocean to the Philippine Islands. I thought Floy must miss the ocean and the islands she lived on. When she pushed me in the hammock she sang,

Reuben, Reuben, I've been thinking what a grand world this would be,
If all the boys and all the girls could live across the great blue sea.

That song made me want to cross the ocean and explore lands far away, just like Floy had done.

"Janie," Floy said, telling me another tale, "one time I took a train across America to Los Angeles, California, to get to the Philippines to marry my Fred. And I wasn't yet 20 years old." She looked sad all of a sudden. "Our first babies were twins, but they were born dead."

Floy had three other children, but when she came home to America she had to leave her twin babies in Manila. She called the city they lived in "Vanilla Manila" because the tropical flowers there had a sweet aroma.

Floy told me another story, one about my Uncle Garner.

"When Garner was three years old he ran away from our home in Manila," she said. "The American army spent a day and a half looking for him."

"Did they find him?" I asked.

"Oh, yes," she said. "They found him sitting on a dock at the port of Manila. He had a paper pad in his lap full of drawings he had made of the different ships in port."

Floy was quiet. Then she said, with a smile, "Garner was precocious."

"What does that mean?" I asked

"It means, *before your time.*"

I wanted to be before my time.

I stopped swinging, walked back to the house, and tiptoed inside. In the kitchen I opened the ice box. It was full of food. I peeked in Daddy's door to make sure he was still asleep. I went to the cupboard, pulled out wax paper, and packed a picnic supper of turkey leg, bread pudding with raisins, and leftover field peas. I put the food in a brown paper bag, then slipped out the back door, and ran to the garage. I put the food in the basket of my bicycle, climbed on, and pedaled toward the tracks.

When I reached the train tracks, I paused and thought about what I was doing. Mama and Daddy told me never to cross the tracks alone. Then I thought about Sam's watery eyes — and about Floy's adventures — and I kept right on pedaling. The road across the tracks was not covered with oyster shells like Camp Avenue; it was muddy and rutted. It was hard to pedal. I got off and pushed my bike.

At a tar-paper shack on one corner I saw a woman, her head wrapped in a bright kerchief, hanging clothes on a line stretched between two trees. Children ran around her feet.

She looked up and saw me. She stopped hanging clothes.

"Where's Ole Sam?" I asked.

"Child, you better get back across them tracks right now." She put her hands on her hips. "You ain't got no business over here. And none with Sam neither."

"But I've got something for him," I said. "Where does he live?"

"Sam don't stay nowhere in particular. He sleeps where night time find him."

"He doesn't have a house?"

"That's right. Now you get on home yourself!"

"I have some food for him."

"God Almighty, Child, you full of obstination."

Then she pointed a bony finger across the alley to a dilapidated barn. I walked toward the barn and saw Sam standing against the fence post with his back to me. He didn't hear me approach, so I pulled on his shirt tail.

"I brought you something to eat."

"You shouldn't be 'cross them tracks, Missy. You better get on home. Your daddy might put some blames on me."

I held out the sack to him. "Don't you want the food?"

He didn't reply. Sam just stood still and quiet, staring out into the blue of the late afternoon sky. Then he pointed toward the barn, "Just put the sack in there. I eat it shortly."

The barn was filled with hay. I looked around for a table, but there was nothing, just straw. I placed the paper bag on top of a pile of straw and went outside to my bike.

"Bye, Sam," I called out.

He tipped his worn hat.

I pushed my bike to the tracks as fast as I could, crested the railway hill, then jumped on my bike and pedaled home. As I put up my bike in the garage, Mama and Floy arrived home. Floy went right to the ice box to start supper.

"Where is my turkey leg?"

I said nothing.

"Janie, did you eat the turkey leg?"

"No, Ma'am."

"Did your daddy eat it?"

"No, Ma'am."

"Well, did the leg go walking off by itself?"

Frightened, I ran to Floy and threw my arms around her waist.

"Oh, Floy, I did something terrible today! I went across the tracks all by myself." I started to cry.

I felt her body stiffen. She pushed me away to look me in the eyes.

"We're outta sight ten minutes and you go and do something like that! You better have a good reason, young lady, or you are in serious trouble."

"I do have a good reason," I sobbed. "Daddy wouldn't give Ole Sam any food so I took him some. He was hungry."

"You did what!?"

"I took Sam your turkey leg and some bread puddin'. And some peas."

"Janie, Janie, Janie," she said, shaking her head. "What am I going do with you? God may be color blind, but your daddy certainly isn't. He's gonna have a conniption when he finds out what you've done."

"I'm sorry, Floy. Please don't tell Daddy," I pleaded.

Floy put her arms around me and snuggled me against her full soft breasts.

"It's all right," she said. "You did the right thing, just not the safe thing." Floy stroked my hair. "Sometimes they are different."

I sat quietly with Floy for a while. Then I began to wonder if Sam was safe sleeping in the barn.

"Floy, did you know that Ole Sam doesn't have a house?"

"Sure he does, Janie. He lives with his daughter. Samantha."

"No," I said, "he sleeps in a barn."

"Janie, are you sure? I think he lives with Samantha."

"No, he lives in a barn with straw piled up in it. He showed me. And besides, a woman over there told me he sleeps wherever night time finds him."

"Mercy!" Floy said, letting out a deep breath. "There are heathens among us now. In a barn!"

Floy was upset. She told me to run outside and play until supper time. I went outside for a minute, then I slipped back inside and hid behind the kitchen door. I watched Floy take off her apron and go to the clothes closet in the hall. She put on her going-somewhere-important straw hat, plopped it on her head, and fastened it with a hat pin. She went to the linen cabinet and took down a stack of freshly ironed sheets and her good comforter, the one she saved for company. Floy tied the package together with a string. With the package under one arm and her purse on her shoulder, Floy walked out the door and turned toward the railroad tracks.

Floy was kind. Floy always did the right thing.

But I was beginning to figure out she didn't always do the safe thing.

Me, my mother, and Harriet

4

The screened porch at our Camp Avenue house opened into the living room which opened onto the dining room which opened on to the breakfast room and kitchen. The dining room with Floy's huge oak table, which easily served twelve, was the heart of our home, the place for Sunday dinners and entertaining guests.

I liked to hide under the table, lean against the large center post, and listen to the adults talk.

The day of my third birthday, my mother took one of Harriet's cast-off pink dresses, which Harriett had refused to wear, hemmed it up, and squeezed my chubby body into it. The dress made me feel like a princess. I was excited about my upcoming birthday party. Mama and Floy talked about making a cake but having to use ration cards to purchase the extra sugar.

"Floy," I asked, "what is a rash-on card. Is it like a birthday card?"

"No, Honey," she said, "it gives us permission to buy sugar, leather shoes, or gasoline for the car."

I didn't understand, but as long as I had a cake with pink icing I didn't care.

That special Saturday morning, Harriet came in from playing outside and put her baseball bat and ball on top of my side of the bed.

"Move your stuff!" I yelled. "That's my side!"

I thought since it was my birthday Harriet might be nice.

"Just because you are gonna be three," she sneered, "doesn't make you special. You are still fat, you brat."

I knew better than to tell Mama what Harriet said because she wouldn't believe me. I sulked. I hid under the table and crunched the pink dress into a wad.

Soon Daddy, Harriet, Floy, and Papa came to the dining room to greet two strange men who had just come in the front door. They were soldiers boarding at Myrtie Evans' house across the street. The soldiers wore uniforms. I didn't know them and did not want them at my party, so I stayed under the table. One of the soldiers leaned down and looked at me.

"Hi, birthday girl," he said, "can you come out from your hiding place? We brought you a present."

I climbed out from under the table. "What is the present?" I asked.

"Well, come here and we'll help you open it."

"I don't need any help to open presents!" I shouted as I grabbed the gift. I unwrapped it and threw the gift paper on the floor. A book fell out. The cover had a shiny red and green picture on the front. I rubbed the smooth cover against my cheek.

"Floy, look!" I said, "It's a book all my own!"

"Yes," she said. "Mind your manners. Thank these nice gentlemen for your present. This afternoon we will read it."

I murmured, "Thanks." Then I asked, "But Floy, what is the book called?"

Floy read the cover. *Little Sally Mandy*. And look," she said, "she is holding a box with a kitty cat in it. Oh, this will be so fun to read!"

When it was time to cut the cake and serve the ice cream, Mama let me climb on top of the table. I sat right next to my cake. Mama let me lick the pink icing from around the bottom of the cake. The icing tasted better than butter!

Floy suggested we sing "Happy Birthday" before cutting the cake. I sang as fast as I could, ahead of the others, hoping to get to the cake sooner than later. Floy cut the biggest piece for me. Mama had to wipe the icing from around my mouth.

"You will be pink all over if you are not careful," she whispered. I didn't care.

After we had cake and vanilla, homemade ice cream, my daddy gave me a box wrapped in pretty white paper. Inside was a tin dog on wheels that had a red leash attached. I climbed off the table, put the dog on the wooden floor and pulled him around. The dog barked!

"Oh," I shrieked. I hoped this day would never end.

As the soldiers were preparing to leave, one of them leaned over, twisted my nose, and said, "Someday when those freckles go away you will be a pretty little girl."

Everyone laughed.

Except me.

5

My parents sent me to a private first grade in the home of Mrs.
Bouslog — a gray-faced, white-haired woman. Class was held in her home.
A house painted dark red. Her windows were covered with blinds creating
a dark, oppressive environment.

After my first day in Mrs. Bouslog's home school, I refused to return. My mother cajoled. She threatened. She bribed me. But I was adamant.
Learning was not for me.

The next day, Daddy and Mama, together, got me in the car. Arriving at school, Mama and Mrs. Bouslog dragged me out of the car while I
kicked and screamed. They carried me into the house, Mama at my arms,
Mrs. Bouslog toting my feet. As soon as they put me down on her floor,
Mama hurried out. Mrs. Bouslog slammed the door and stood in front of
it, while I kicked and screamed in a tantrum. I finally quit crying only because
my throat hurt worse than my feelings. Reluctantly, I stood up and went and
sat in the circle of students.

There were nineteen other five-year-old children besides me at the
home school. First thing every morning, we were made to sit at tables to
color butterflies. I despised butterflies. I colored them black and brown,
making them as ugly as possible.

The old gray-haired hag with a bun stood behind me.

"Stay in the lines! It isn't hard. Anyone can do it."

In the learning circle, all twenty of us learned the alphabet, sight
words, and to read "See Spot Run. See Jane Run."

The other children laughed and taunted me saying, "The book Jane is prettier than you, Jane!"

Mrs. Bousalog did nothing to stop the teasing.

I didn't learn to read as fast as the others. And I refused to answer any of the teacher's questions. One morning I wet my pants while in the learning circle. Again, the children laughed. Mrs. Bouslog scolded me for getting her chair wet.

I threatened to run away if Mama made me go back to school, but she and Daddy insisted. The next day, they forcibly put me in the car. When we arrived at school, Mama took off the new watch Daddy had given her for her birthday and asked me to wear it for her to protect it.

I reasoned if I took the watch and wore it, Mama would change her mind, come back to get the watch, then I could jump in the car to escape.

The strategy failed me. Mama did not come back for the watch, but she did appear at noon when school was over to pick me up. I reached across the car seat to return her watch, proud I had not broken it.

Days, weeks, and months went by. First grade was torture. At play time I was bullied. Praise for any effort to learn was a foreign commodity. But I realized I was in a losing a battle. Mama and Floy were both teachers. To them, learning was everything. When the two of them finally understood I was miserable in school, they encouraged me more, tutored me more often, and praised my efforts. I gave in.

Mrs. Bouslog planned a parents' gathering — a party — for the evening before Christmas break. Our holiday gift to our parents was to read a story to them. I was still a poor reader and dreaded that night. All too soon it arrived. After refreshments, we were told to find places to sit so we could read to the parents. Mama, Daddy, and I went out on the front porch. We sat in a squeaky glider. Mrs. Bouslog handed me a thick book to read. I had never seen it before.

I started to cry.

Daddy got up, went into the classroom, and came back with a book he and I had read together entitled *The Little Purple Pup*. He handed me the book and grinned all the while I read. Mrs. Bouslog came to the porch to inquire about my skill in reading. She obviously did not notice we had switched books. She looked directly at Daddy and asked if I had read the book.

Mama looked down at the floor.

"Yep," he said, "and she did it darn well."

Mrs. Bouslog then gave Daddy a silver bar pin to place on my collar. After that night, Daddy often let me sit in his lap and read him a book. When I stumbled on a word he said, "That old word shouldn't be in there . . . at least not for little five year old girls wantin' to read."

During the second semester I caught on. I embraced reading and became quite competent, even when asked to read aloud to the group. I spent hours at home on our screen porch perched in our hammock reading book after book. My Grandmother Floy praised me and often made her special pecan pralines for me. Reading led to sweets. I read a lot!

In May, the entire first grade planned a May Day celebration. A swimming party. We were told we could wear our bathing suits for the whole day. Mine was too tight and made lines across my butt but I was so excited about getting to swim I didn't care. At school, mid-morning we were instructed to go outside and get in our May Day circle. We held hands and went round and round the May Pole laughing and jumping for joy knowing we would soon be swimming.

Suddenly, we were hit with a strong spray of hose water. We ran and hid behind bushes and on low magnolia limbs. The stream kept coming. Mrs. Bouslog took aim and soaked us all. There was no swimming pool for our class.

If I ever became a teacher like Floy and Mama, I would make learning fun, exciting, and I would not tell lies to my students.

Learning would not take place in a dark room.

Me (back row,, center) at The May Day "swimming" celebration
at Mrs. Bouslog's first grade school.

6

My sister Harriet spent her time outside playing badminton, baseball or football with our neighbors Joe, Ed, and Jerry. She was a tomboy. Sports were her domain. Our house was mine. I roamed from room to room hiding in clothes closets or linen cabinets while I spied on Floy and Papa. Sometimes they kissed and laughed. Sometimes I heard Floy read the Psalms to Papa while he packed or unpacked his valise. They held hands and prayed together.

I memorized some of Floy's favorite Psalm 23. She was surprised when I quoted several verses.

She patted me on the head and said, "Janie, there's a marvelous brain inside of your head."

Floy never called me "stupid" like Harriet and her friends did.

On Sunday afternoons, I hid under our dining room table. Scrunched up under there I watched as Mama danced around the room. She hummed along with the orchestra on the radio's *Longine Whittenhaur Hour*.

Mama thought music was what God let us take with us when he chased us out of Eden. While Mama danced and hummed, Daddy slept and snored on the plaid davenport. When Mama's siblings Aunt Vi or Uncle Garner visited us I hid behind the living room's velvet curtains to listen to their conversations.

Uncle Garner and Aunt Vi smoked cigarettes, against Floy's wishes, as they told more stories about living in London and Calcutta.

Uncle Garner and Aunt Vi

Uncle Garner wrote articles about war-torn England and Europe for the *National Geographic* magazine. He also invented a small powerboat for the British Army — a boat that could be powered by human waste.

He built a prototype inside his flat on the Thames River. Army men came to test its seaworthiness, but Uncle Garner had constructed the boat too large to move out through his door. He rebuilt it outside. The Army came again and placed the boat in the river. It sank.

Aunt Vi was one of the early female law graduates from the University of Mississippi. Before she began to practice law, she sailed on an army troop ship through the China Sea in order to get to India to help feed and clothe those in need. After being in Calcutta for several months she was transferred to a remote post thirty miles from any large city. While in the rural area, a wild chimpanzee bit her while she was sleeping. She had to stay in a hospital tent for there were no available doctors. Her co-workers gave her shots, treated her fever, and prayed for her. She was soon well but asked to be returned to Calcutta.

After a family lunch, Daddy and Harriet seldom stayed at the dining table to visit. They went out to the garage to hammer and saw. They built wooden chairs for our lawn or repaired my swing, or Harriet's sliding board. Mama, Floy, Papa, Vi and Garner sat at the table for hours sharing stories and eating what was left of Floy's shrimp gumbo and boiled crabs. I stayed hidden. I listened and imagined going on adventures like my aunt and uncle.

Hiding was the best part of my days.

The James and Stanley Family on Camp Avenue in Gulfport.
(L to R): Garner, Elizabeth, Vi, Floy, Harriet, Fred, Jane, Harry

Harriet and me

7

My slow motion days drifted by. I lay on my back on the St. Augustine grass in our front yard to find faces in passing clouds. Often I spent entire mornings in a homemade swing. I swung higher and higher until I built up courage to jump into a pile of crisp, dried oak leaves. I daydreamed about a day when I would join a circus and jump out of a swing to thrill spellbound audiences. Swinging was flying to me. I never tired of back and forth. Sometimes I hid in the purple wisteria bush next to our porch. There, in my own leafy castle, I could be a princess who could hear the conversations of the grownups and visitors.

When Harriet wanted me to come out of hiding, she threw acorns or pecans at me. She made me cry. Harriet liked being rough. She didn't play the piano or take dancing lessons. She didn't sing in the First Baptist Church children's choir like I did, and she never ate sugar on her butter sandwiches.

To teach me responsibility, Mama or Floy asked me to do helpful chores. When they got too busy grading papers, they sent me on errands. I felt important when I walked across the vacant lot to Mrs. Kelsall's house to buy fresh garden parsley for gumbo, or to Mrs. Schloegel's, who was my friend, Georgie's mama, for fresh vegetables. Sometimes I walked with Floy across the railroad tracks to Rich's Grocery Store to buy sliced bread. We passed Mrs. Stevens' yard which had a statue of a lady in a blue robe holding a naked baby boy. Floy said it was a heathen practice to have an idol of the Virgin Mary standing there among the boxwood plants and flowering azaleas for the whole world to see. Even though I could tell Floy didn't approve of that statue, she reminded me the Lord God and Jesus wanted us to treat Catholics as if they, too, belonged to the First Baptist Church. So we did. When Mrs. Stevens' gout sprouted, Floy cooked special buttered egg custard for her and sat a spell on the porch for a visit. They didn't talk church talk. Secretly I was glad when Mrs. Stevens' gout flared up. I got to lick the egg custard cook pot.

When we reached Rich's Grocery, Floy said, "Youngsters must always open doors for their elders." She instructed me to pull open the screen door with the smooth blue and orange Colonial Bakery handles so she could go in first. Entering the darkened, fan-cooled cavern with creaking wooden floors was like walking into Aladdin's cave of treasures. The shelves were stacked high with Moon Pies, marshmallows, and five-cent brown-bottled Orange Crush. There were aisles of wooden tables and crates stacked with pyramids of apples, oranges, bananas, turnips, tomatoes and silver tasseled corn. The aroma of Rich's was a warm blend of shucked corn, over-ripe cantaloupes, and fresh pine sawdust on the floor. The store buzzed with the hum of iridescent winged flies. Floy kept our icebox filled with fresh fish, shrimp, and crabs we caught ourselves and chickens and eggs gathered from our own hen house. We usually only bought things at Rich's we couldn't supply ourselves, like toilet tissue and Spam for when Daddy was home.

Daddy grew up in West Point, Mississippi and didn't eat seafood. Mother teased him about being a northerner.

Aside from errands, I had other chores as well. I polished the icebox with appliance wax and dried the dinner plates whose pattern featured a blue pagoda in the center.

My favorite chore was to dry and put the silverware in the drawer.

I pretended the forks were beautiful maidens. I danced and twirled them from the sink to the utility drawer.

Knives were sharp-jawed men who were elegant, yet feared. I took special care drying each knife before placing it into the proper slot in the drawer.

Spoons were chubby and unimportant, enviously watching the waltz of the forks and knives. I dumped the spoons all together, still damp, into the drawer.

They reminded me . . . of me.

8

My world was dominated by attentive, overachieving females. Mama and Floy were school teachers. The men in my life were absent, both physically and emotionally. Daddy worked for the Mississippi Power Company as a traveling accountant. My granddaddy, Papa, a civil engineer for the government, caught the Hummingbird L&N train to New Orleans every Sunday evening.

The men returned home each weekend, but during the week ours was a houseful of women — me, my sister Harriet (older than me by three years, which she never let me forget), Mama and Floy.

I awoke most mornings to the sing song chants of the *Oyyy-ster Maaannn from Pass Christiaaannn*. Spring and summer dawns, he pushed his wobbly wooden wheelbarrow up the road's slight incline selling freshly caught blue crabs, shrimp, trout, and oysters, depending on the season. His chants were accompanied by the squeaks of the iron wheel of the barrow as it scraped along the oyster shell road. The salty, odious aroma of the *crème de la mare* surrounded the barrow.

From my single bed in the tiny front room of our house I could hear Floy hasten outside, coins jingling in her apron pocket, to purchase the fresh "treasures of the sea" as she called the food we ate every day except Saturday and Sunday when Daddy was home.

At home, females ran things.

Conversely, worship at the First Baptist Church was dominated by men — the preacher, the choir director, and the deacons. Our preacher hollered so loudly, I assumed he was trying either to make sure God heard him or he was awfully mad about something.

Southern Baptists believed in separation of boys and girls. Separate Sunday School classes. Separate times to swim in the pool. No dancing. And certainly no kissing.

Dr. Chester Swore, a visiting evangelist, came to our church to lecture our youth group. The boys and girls were in separate lectures. Dr. Swore told us girls never to wear red dresses because ladies in red were promiscuous, obviously inviting Satan to lead them into sin. Holding hands or hugging was not just a forbidden act, it was a sin. He reported he had recently been at a high school where a boy and girl were walking across campus holding hands. He went right up to them and looked them in the eye.

"Stop that immediately!" he scolded. "What are you saving for marriage!?"

To me, boys were untouchable, unapproachable, and different.

I suppose Mama and Floy, being devout Baptists, felt obliged to be silent about sex, thereby passing on the Baptist myth that sex is sin. Sex was never discussed in our home, at least not within my hearing.

I was completely ignorant. However, I learned fascinating things about sex from Cynthia. Since her daddy was a doctor, she was an expert on body matters. When I was eight years old, I rushed in my house crying, demanding that Mama hurry off to Woolworth's to buy me a bra.

That day Cynthia told me that if I didn't start wearing a bra immediately my breasts would grow as long as my arms. I believed everything Cynthia told me was true because she ended all her explanations with "if you don't believe me, just go ask my daddy." It made all her proclamations seem plausible.

When I was eleven years old, the menses came upon me. It felt like a death knell.

Sweaty from playing Piggy Wants A Signal, I ran home to go to the bathroom. When I pulled down my panties, I noticed blood. I couldn't imagine how I cut myself *there*.

"Mama! Mama!" I cried. "Come quick! I'm bleeding!"

Mama came, took a quick look, and all but chanted, "Janie is a woman! Janie is a woman!"

With that, Mama handed me a huge cotton pad with an elastic belt and showed me how to put it on.

"This thing is disgusting! I can't run and climb with this bandage stuck between my legs. Can't you make the bleeding stop?"

"Oh, don't worry. It only happens four or five days a month."

"You mean this will happen again?!"

Determined not to let this revolting development completely destroy me, I remembered Floy telling me that blue astringent ST-37 could make almost any sore disappear. I got the bottle down from the medicine cabinet and threw large handfuls of the stinging liquid onto my bottom, but it did not stop the flow of rapidly advancing womanhood.

Depressed, yet still optimistic about a possible redemption from this curse, I went outside and tried to pretend I was riding the Kotex like I rode an imaginary horse. It was horribly uncomfortable. As I attempted to gallop with this new burden between-my-legs, I came upon a distressing sight. I watched four men with a tar truck and a tractor begin to pave the shell road in front of my house.

I ran to the curb and yelled, "Stop! Stop! Please don't pave our road. You'll ruin it!"

It was a meaningless plea. Because of the gush of uninvited maturity, I saw a future with no more tree climbing, no more running unencumbered through Bailey Woods or on the beach. And now, no more warm, squishy rain filled mud puddles! No more dams and swishing currents to chase to the gulf. These losses were more than I could bear. In desolation, I went inside my house and climbed in my bed. I hid under the covers and cried myself to sleep.

9

The same year they paved Camp Avenue, the Fants bought an air conditioning unit. I lost access to my friends and neighbors. My entire life, Cynthia, Joe, Janice, Ed, Kay Minor, Nancy, Harriet, and I had freely run in and out of each others' houses, as comfortable in one mama's kitchen as another's.

Then one by one my neighbors closed windows. They shut doors. They lowered shades. They installed noisy boxes onto window frames to cool the interior of their homes. For the first time in my life, I had to knock on a door and wait for it to be opened. I sat in rooms, once light and breezy, now cool but dark. Our conversations were louder so our voices could carry over the whirring of the air conditioning motors.

And then another box infiltrated Gulfport. Our neighborhood evening gatherings on front porches and in backyards stopped all together. Our camaraderie vied against Imogene Coco, Milton Berle, Ed Sullivan, and Friday night boxing. Television pulled my friends away from me. It tantalized and scandalized and whetted appetites for weekly episodes of comedy or tragedy. I felt betrayed; I could not compete.

As I sat barefooted in the morning dew and looked across a concrete road to shut tight houses with rectangular protrusions and tall antennae on the rooftops, I felt the loss of simple friendships. I was more alone than I had ever been before.

Janice and Cynthia did not understand why I was upset, but as friends do, they came over to console me. Janice had just returned from

Woolworth's where she had spent her clothing allowance on a garter belt. She brought it over for me to see. She explained its use, but it looked to me more like an octopus than a piece of clothing. I wondered why anyone would willingly wear such a contraption and I asked Janice exactly that. She told me it was to hold up stockings. I thought about Floy rolling her thick flesh-brown cotton hose and tying them in a knot above her knees. Mama wore a girdle when she wore stockings.

When I told Janice of these simplified ways to hold up stockings, she informed me that there were only two kinds of ladies in the whole world: those who wore girdles and those who were garter belts. She further declared that only those ladies who wore garter belts ever had any fun!

My poor Mama. Since I knew she would never wear such a contraption, I figured she must be faking her laughter. I knew I would never wear that thing either. I wondered what would happen to me when fun wasn't an option.

• • •

Janice, Cynthia, and Martha Ann all got interested in boys a long time before Jackie and I did, but then they were not Baptists. Presbyterians and Methodists must have been taught a different Adam and Eve story from the Baptist version. I could not understand what all the fuss was about. Boys to me were just strange looking creatures who peed standing up. They were also convenient when we wanted to play softball. All in all, they seemed to be an argumentative bunch. Nonetheless, when Janice went to the movies to meet Billy, I tagged along with her. She and I spent a nickel of our allowance to ride the bus to downtown Gulfport. We strolled down two blocks to Woolworth's counter for a hamburger and malt before meeting Billy at the Paramount Theater. Every Saturday morning the theater showed Westerns where I learned men in white were good and black-clothed men were evil. I usually saved a nickel to buy popcorn. I smacked on it while I became enamored with Trigger and less so, Roy Rogers.

When we sat down in the darkened theater, Billy reached over and grabbed Janice's hand and held it between their two boxes of popcorn. I could not watch the beginning of the movie because I knew it was my duty to pray for their poor, lost souls. According to Dr. Swore, holding hands was paramount to having illegal babies.

When I finished praying, the movie had begun. I watched the remainder with smug foreknowledge that the good men in white would surely win their struggle over the bad men in black. As the credits rolled, I sighed with comfort and relief over the naive justice of it all.

When we left the theater though, I couldn't help noticing that Billy was dressed primarily in black.

10

While it is true I was a frumpy, chubby, frizzy-headed child and adolescent, somehow, miraculously, I blossomed in high school. I had longed to be tall and slim, and now I was. At 5'9" I stood taller than almost all of the girls and even some of the boys. I don't recall how it happened. Maybe it was all the dancing lessons Mama insisted I take.

Along with my high school peers, I read *Gone with the Wind* and marked the risqué pages. Bewitched by Rhett Butler, I yearned to watch more sophisticated movies and eventually television soap operas where love and sex were routine. I struggled to keep up the Baptist code of ethics and tried hard to avoid being interested in such evil matters as relationships with boys and holding hands and dancing. I did just fine until I began a long-term dance with Neil White, Jr., sometimes a lilting waltz, more often than not, a tangled tango of two.

Of all the boys in our class, Neil was perhaps the most different from me, at least in background and family. He was rich; we were not. His parents enjoyed cocktails (his dad lots of them); mine did not touch alcohol. His family did not attend church; mine never missed a Sunday. He cussed, drank, smoked — and he laughed at religious dogma. Yet there was something about him that called out to me in a way I had never experienced before.

At age sixteen, I did not often date. Rumor had it I was a D.D.H. (Damn Door Hanger). When Neil called to invite me on a date, I thought he might have been dared to do so by Robbie Webb, Bill Touchstone, or

My junior yearbook photo

Johnny Martin, all of whom had asked me out only once. The repeat dates were never forthcoming because I would not stop hanging on my door so as not to slide over the seat to snuggle with the boy while he drove with one hand and groped with the other.

Neil arrived at my house in his daddy's fin-tailed, white Cadillac convertible with the top down. The front floor under the glove compartment was taken up by a set-in air conditioner blowing full blast into the open air. There was no place for my feet except curled up under me. With the top down, my long hair blowing tornadoes around my face and head, we drove to Fairchild's Restaurant on the beach for dinner. I'd never been out to dinner with a date and feared I might over order. I searched the menu for a cheap entree. I asked for a baked potato with butter. Neil read the menu cover to cover. Unable to decide between the sirloin steak with baked potato and the fried shrimp with fries, he ordered both. He ate them both, then ordered dessert — a piece of key lime pie and a bowl of ice cream.

As we left the restaurant he hollered over his shoulder to the waitress, "Charge it to my mama, please, and don't forget to add a tip."

We left the restaurant and drove to Biloxi. Neil paid a $2 cover charge for us to enter the Slovenian Lodge to dance to the music of the Red Tops from Vicksburg. Neil was a smooth dancer and was easy to follow. We jitter-bugged to Elvis' "Blue Suede Shoes" and swayed to Fats Domino's "Blueberry Hill." As we slow danced to "Love Me Tender" and the Platter's "Only You," I tried to keep a Baptist distance between us, but I never knew what to do with my cheek when it kept bumping into his horn-rimmed glasses. Neil took his pointer finger, straightened his glasses, and pulled me close again.

My curfew was 10 pm. We arrived home at 11 pm. My daddy was outside propped up on the brick stoop waiting for us.

When Neil opened the door for me, Daddy said to him, "Boy, you're late bringing my daughter home. You probably thought we'd have breakfast waiting for you."

Neil turned to shake Daddy's hand. "I'm sorry Mr. Stanley. It won't happen again. I promise."

Daddy didn't shake his hand, rather he put his arm around Neil's shoulder and said, "You durn right it won't happen again. Now get on home!"

Being a D.D.H., getting home late, and being scolded by Daddy, I knew that was the first and last date I would have with Neil. I was wrong.

Daddy did not scare Neil off. Neil courted and entertained me.

And he was fun. We laughed together over silly things. I could bend the top knuckle of my little finger and wiggle it up and down so fast it looked like it was not attached to my finger. I'd flipped it in front of Neil's face. He said he saw a Watusi Witch do that one time. I liked being called Watusi. He made it sound funny.

Neil was on the Gulfport High School's golf team with Mary Mills, his next-door neighbor. She was such a gifted golfer she played on the boy's team. However, when other schools protested about playing with a girl on the team, Gulfport had to develop its own girls' team. Mary asked me if I would join the team so she could continue to play.

"Yes," I said, "but I don't know how to play."

"Don't worry," she said, "I can handle it."

Mary recruited two other team members who were nearly as inexperienced as I. The very first time I ever held a golf club was in a high school tournament. Mary was my partner. We won. Mary shot a 34 on 9 holes.

Neil became my golf coach. We played at the Great Southern Country Club and at Sunkist Club. After my lessons we would go to the snack bar for hamburgers and French fries. Often, we stayed late and rode in a golf cart all over the courses so I could become familiar with the different holes, the water hazards, and the sand traps. I enjoyed riding in the cart with Neil. The courses were beautiful with large oaks and palm trees lining each hole. Occasionally, I felt drowsy and would lean back to rest. I learned not to do that. Neil liked bringing me back to alertness by speeding the golf cart up and down and into ditches. Twice, we nearly turned over.

In the evenings, we would go to his house to swim. Their pool was the largest on the coast. We swam, dove, turned somersaults, and kissed under water. On weekends, we often took a small boat out to Cat Island or Ship Island with our friends, George Schloegel and Peggy Jay Harry.

One day, as we approached the island, George told me to throw over the anchor. I did. It was not tied to the boat. Unexpected swims were necessary on some of the outings.

Neil was a sharp dresser and liked to dress up when we went out on a date. He also liked to dance. He bought a portable record player, which was rare for the day. On summer evenings we would take the record player and our favorite records to the yacht club, would walk out on the pier, and have our own dance party under a moon-lit sky.

Our togetherness began to seem natural, while other parts of my life felt strange, unappealing. We grew closer and closer together. When we were not together, I took the home phone into the middle bedroom of our house, stretched the cord out as far as possible, curled up in the corner and whispered my conversations with Neil so my parents couldn't hear me.

Neil had a sarcastic wit, yet he was always a southern gentleman around females. But it was a well-known fact that he was a rascal around his male counterparts. That was the Neil I fell in love with. He challenged me in ways that often made me uncomfortable, like wanting me to smoke a cigarette with him, or sip on his beer, or stay out later than was allowed.

During my senior year of high school I struggled between the pull of my relationship with Neil and my Baptist code. The biblical *Love your fellow man, lay down your life for a friend, love is the most important thing in all of life, do not have sex or you will die and burn in Hell forever and ever, Amen* was firmly embedded in me. I believed in the literal meaning of each and every bible verse, so it was difficult for me to meld together the verses which stood in opposition to each other. Neil did not have this struggle.

Neil came from a family of wealth, intrigue, alcoholism, and overindulgence. His mother Martha, a Vassar college girl who was heir to the Borg Warner fortune, had married an irascible high school senior. They met at a dance on the roof of the Markham Hotel. On a whim, they paid a friend, Buck Heiss, to drive them to Pascagoula so they could elope that same night. When they returned from Pascagoula where they married, they went to Martha's home in Edgewater Park to tell her mother she had just married Neil White. Her mother gasped in disbelief. Her step father, according to family lore, the old ship Captain Ritchie, exposed himself.

Martha was one of the most kind and thoughtful women I'd ever met. Her husband, Neil Sr., a self-proclaimed socialite even though he was now married, never stopped his drinking and womanizing. His friends named him "Old Dog."

My Neil — Neil Jr. — was the oldest of their six children. In the eighth grade he fell at a camp at Walloon Lake, Michigan, and broke his back, losing 2-3 inches of height. Neil, Jr. had dark hair and blue eyes. He wore horn-rimmed glasses. His shoulders were broad even though he stood with a slight stoop. His smile was crooked, more open to the left than the right. His usual demeanor was of a cool guy with a caustic attitude and sarcastic wit. We were different in almost too many ways. Yet, in spite of our differences, or perhaps because of them, we were more than just attracted to one another.

I loved Neil with all the knowledge and compassion that a sheltered seventeen year old could possess.

Some afternoons after school we drove to the Park and Eat, ordered French fries with ketchup, talked about our friends and his golf scores. Occasionally we went to either my house or his for supper. I adored Neil and the time we spent together.

The only love role model I had was my mother, who offered a life-saving succor to the world. I emulated her and morphed into a mothering entity, more a correcting presence to Neil than a girlfriend.

I was a controlling influence on the once free-wheeling, easygoing Neil, Jr. He often received detention for being late to school, getting drunk at school functions, not turning in homework, failing tests or sleeping in class. I attempted to protect him from himself, cornering him in the hall to tell him to spit out his gum, or to get his homework done, or to help him study for tests. At first he was amenable to my manipulative actions.

Then his buddies started mocking me.

Ooooh Neilie, they would say, *spit out your gum* or *Hi, Sweetie, did you do your Latin? Can you conjugate your verbs?*

Neil rebelled. He found subtle ways to maintain his bad boy image (his "giving the finger" slipped through the editors and sponsors of the annual and it was printed in our yearbook).

Our high school dating was the first step in a sixteen year roller coaster journey of two young souls seeking the transformative power love had promised.

In the 1950s nice Baptist girls would not allow boys to touch them at all, much less the breast area. But, like most other boys in our high school, that seemed to be the area that most interested Neil.

As time progressed, the "body me" began to feel rich with adoration for Neil. The "rational me" thought I was headed straight for Hell. I tried to ignore the latter.

On a balmy, late-Spring night, we walked to the beach with an old quilted comforter he kept in his Ford Fairlane. I sacrificed my Baptist belief of hell and damnation in the name of love.

• • •

Neil's family, all eight of the Whites and their two servants, Wash and Ester, embraced me, and I each one of them. Wash and Ester lived in

Beside my 1957 high school yearbook photo,
the editors wrote: "what she thinks no one knows."

a pool house apartment behind the White's Edgewater Park home. They did the work necessary to keep the family going. None of the family themselves seemed to have any great responsibilities. The children played through the days with very little guidance, no chores to do, no homework help, and no role models in how to be self-reliant and unselfish. There was little daily structure in their household. Each day, it seemed, held its own peculiarity, challenge and chaos. My own household was consistently routine and predictable. My home was neat and orderly with every item in its proper place.

Neil needed my family's stability. I needed his family's spontaneity.

During June through August, the White family spent summers in the cool climate of Walloon Lake, Michigan, in their six-bedroom two-story log cabin. Servants catered to them while they swam, fished, skied, sailed, rode horses, dined out and partied with other teenagers, children of American business's top CEOs. My senior year, I went to Walloon Lake with the Whites for two weeks. I was invited by Neil's young friends to go for a weekend shopping spree to a place called D'Leone's. It was in Paris, France. I declined. J.C. Penney was upscale for me.

While in college, Neil and I discussed marriage. However, my daddy said I could not get married until I finished school. I had completed my freshman year at Mississippi State College for Women. That summer I attended Perkinston Junior College and took four more college courses. Then I transferred to Gulf Park College, attended class there while I took 30 hours of correspondence courses from Ole Miss. I only lacked one semester to graduate. Daddy relented. Neil and I married on August 15, 1959.

The White's social friends wined and dined us at party after party. *The Daily Herald* newspaper reported on every event.

His family wanted a large wedding and a booze-filled reception at the Country Club. With my frugal daddy paying the bills, I knew that would not happen.

We married and had the reception at the First Baptist Church of Gulfport.

At a wedding party (L to R): Neil White, Sr., Martha Johnson White, Neil White, Jr., me, Harry Stanley and Elizabeth Stanley

ONE

11

We honeymooned at Arrowhead, the White family cabin at Walloon Lake. I painted, wrote poetry, and swam in the frigid waters. Neil played golf and sailed with his friends. It was like camp.

In September we moved into the married-students apartment at Ole Miss. We graduated, and stayed in Oxford for three years for Neil to go to law school and for me to earn a Masters in Sociology. During those years I continued to attend a Baptist Church. Alone. Neil opted to play Sunday golf. It distressed me that church was not a priority with Neil. But I had known that before we married. I didn't make an issue of it. But I wished our priorities were more aligned.

Being from the Gulf Coast, a port city and an extension of New Orleans, I was accustomed to cultural offerings. We attended ballets, symphonies, a few operas, formal balls where boas sparkled and tuxedos were common wear, and Sunday brunches on wide verandas where platters of shrimp towered over the table's flower arrangement. By contrast, landlocked, red-clay Oxford was not as stimulating except, of course, in university classes.

Neil and I took a philosophy course entitled *Logic 101* taught by Dr. Van de Vate, a visiting professor from M.I.T. Realizing he would live in Oxford for a year, maybe two, the professor decided to go to the county courthouse to register to vote.

He came to class the following day in a rage.

"I'm leaving Oxford as soon as possible," he said.

When a student asked *why?* he replied, "I'm afraid the bountiful ignorance that graces this place might be a contagious mental illness. My leaving is simply preventative medicine."

"What happened?" another student asked.

Dr. Van de Vate turned red with anger as he related his recent encounter.

"I went to the courthouse. When I got there a clerk told me I had to take the literacy test before I could register. I told her I did not need to take *any* test, especially a literacy test. I pulled out my Phi Beta Kappa key and swung it in front of her face. I shouted, 'This is my Phi Beta Kappa key from M.I.T. It should be obvious I don't need to take a literacy test.'"

"I don't know nothing about no key," the county employee said, "but you got to take the literacy test."

Neil was smart and didn't have to study to make passing grades. He spent his family's money on golf clubs, playing golf, Rebel football games in and out of town, Cutty Sark Scotch, parties at our Avent Acres apartment complex, jazz records, and MG and red Triumph convertibles. In response, I hid dollars for food, toilet paper and textbooks, went to class, wrote more poetry, and scanned the Sears catalog for items not found on the square in Oxford, Mississippi.

On one of my busiest days I asked Neil to go to Tidwell's corner store/service station to buy eggs. He was gone over an hour.

When he returned, he handed me a tiny paper sack with two eggs in it.

"Neil, why did you buy only two eggs?"

"It took me nearly an hour to convince the clerk to sell me two eggs. That dumb ass tried to get me to buy 12 of them."

Neil wrote a nine-cent check for the pair.

In April of 1960, I discovered I was pregnant with our first child. My blood rebelled. I was critically anemic. The prescription for severe anemia was to take a "B-12" shot every third day for the last 2½ months of my pregnancy. I left Neil at Ole Miss and I came home to Mama. She taught school, so I spent my days with Floy and Papa in their cottage near the beach. To stay energized, I walked a mile every day. Floy's cook, Annie, prepared soul food to improve my health. We dined on eggplant with shrimp, spinach cooked ten different ways, fresh garden vegetables, pole-caught trout, and homemade biscuits and cornbread at every noon and supper meal. Breakfast was grits and eggs.

Papa spent his days reading mathematics textbooks, looking for errors he could correct. He also, at age 85, studied Palestinian archaeology by way of correspondence courses. He shared his discoveries about digs and tells with Floy and me every afternoon.

Floy and I sat in wooden rockers as she reminisced and I listened. Her mother, Isabel Jane Welborn Garner, was one of nine children. I never met my great grandmother, but I knew two of her brothers. One born in the late 1860's, the other in the early 1870's.

One brother was Col. Ira Welborn, a Congressional Medal of Honor recipient for his heroics in Cuba during the Spanish American War. He later served in South Africa during the Boer War. I had often visited him with Floy as he lay dying in Long Beach, Mississippi.

The other brother was Uncle Wayne. He served as a Commissioner of Agriculture for the Philippine Islands. He had been a professor at Mississippi A & M.

It was Uncle Wayne who first took Floy to the Philippines to assist his wife, Adele. While there, Floy met Fred James and fell in love. After being in the Philippines for three months, Floy and Adele began their jaunt back to the US. En route, they stopped in Egypt. Fred followed Floy there. Heavily chaperoned by Aunt Adele, Fred plotted to climb the pyramid steps for some time alone with Floy, since Adele would be physically unable to follow. Floy and Fred climbed the giant steps to the very top where he carved

*Fred (far left), Aunt Adele (in black) and Floy (far right)
in Egypt (circa 1903)*

in the sandstone — *Mr. and Mrs. Fred James*. It was his way of proposing. After Egypt, Adele and Floy returned to America and stayed in the Washington, D.C. area where Adele entertained members of capital high society, including her friend, First Lady Mrs. Woodrow Wilson.

Fred mailed Floy money to purchase an engagement ring. Instead, she took the money, bought a train ticket to San Francisco — and then a steamer ship ticket from there to the Philippine Islands.

She braved this trip half way around the world all alone, un-chaperoned at age 20.

As Floy told of these exploits I found her spirit of adventure and fearlessness intoxicating. I wanted to be just like her.

When she arrived in Manila, she and Fred were married and lived there for nine years. My mother Elizabeth, my uncle Garner, and aunt Vi were all born in Manila. When World War I erupted, Fred sent Floy and their three children back to her home state of Mississippi. They settled in Gulfport and rented a house on the beach close to downtown. Floy was hired to be principal of West Ward Elementary School.

Floy could reminisce for hours about her earlier life, but she had a difficult time remembering things present. Her physician diagnosed her with hardening of the arteries. She was excited about becoming a great grandmother. Floy talked often about the coming baby. She knew if I gave birth to a boy he would be named Neil White, III; however, one day, she could not remember the name, but knew it had something to do with the number three.

After a moment she squealed, "Oh, I do remember! His name will be Tertiary!"

Neil, III was born December 5, 1960. He was an 11½ pound, 25 inch long, jaundiced baby boy.

My mother cried, "He is big and beautiful!"

Old Dog squinted at him and said, "Big he is, beautiful he is not."

Me with one-month-old baby Neil

Then, under his breath he added, "Looks like a fat Jap."

The first time Daddy held baby Neil I witnessed a surprising and significant change. Stiff, stoic Daddy softened. Likewise, my gruff sister Harriet became a doting, adoring aunt.

Floy came to our house on Camp Avenue to hold her great-grand-baby as often as possible.

Floy died when baby Neil was two months old. It was almost as if Floy knew cuddling of her first great grandchild would have to last an eternity. At the same time I'd been given the greatest of gifts, I lost the one person who had been a constant source of love and support all my life.

Fearing I would be lost without Floy, I immediately switched my dependence from her to my mother. Mama was ineluctable, dramatic, and subtly controlling. I became her willing puppet.

Soon Baby Neil turned into a blond, blue-eyed precocious child. Husband Neil changed from a 19-year-old, self-centered boy into a caring, overprotective 20-year-old father.

Baby Neil gave me another outlet for my smothering, mothering abilities.

After graduation, I with a Master's Degree in Sociology and Neil with a law degree, we moved back to Gulfport. Over the next few years, Neil practiced law, played golf, and drank whiskey with his friends. He built houses, purchased automobiles, joined the Great Southern Club, the Gulfport Yacht Club, the Century Club, and assorted Mardi Gras krewes. I painted, read books and wrote.

We were parents, acting like adults, but neither of us knew who we were . . . or what we wanted out of life. What we had to offer one another paled in comparison to what we did not have within us to offer.

We joined Westminster Presbyterian Church in Bayou View and became good friends with the young minister and his wife, Frank and Jo-Ann Brooks. Frank took to Neil and encouraged him in his spiritual life.

It felt like the beginning of something wonderful.

12

For three years Neil had been practicing law with his uncle Knox White. There were times when I thought Neil was unhappy with the work. The rigid schedule of representing insurance companies and corporate clients at the law firm didn't suit him.

We dove into church work on the weekends. Neil was elected a deacon. Little Neil was baptized.

Our friendship with the Brooks developed into a closeness that Neil and I both cherished. The four of us cooked dinners for each other, had lunches together, and became dear friends. Frank, aware that Neil was rather new to church and traditional Christian ideas, discussed church history with him. He and Jo-Ann encouraged us to go on a two-week trip to Scotland with them to visit the home land of Presbyterianism.

Since we were going to Europe anyway, Neil's Uncle Knox asked Neil to leave a few days early to take care of a client who lived in Nancy, France. Thrilled at that possibility, I immediately set about to pack and make certain my mother and daddy were available to take care of Neil III. Of course, they were delighted.

In France, Neil and I spent the first two days experiencing Paris as tourists...the Eiffel Tower, the Champs-Elysee, the rose windows of Note-Dame and the panoramic view of the ancient city from the spectacular Sacre-Coeur Cathedral. The Louvre was crowded with tourists, but we managed to see the Mona Lisa and Venus de Milo.

An Arkansas red-neck quickly pointed out to the tour group "that there statue ain't nothing but a concrete woman. We got them in Little Rock!"

The next day we rented a car and drove through the French countryside to Nancy. Neil's meeting took place in a building hundreds of years old and decorated with French antiques. Neither lawyer spoke the others' language but somehow managed to handle the necessary legal documents for Neil to take back home.

We flew from Paris to London to meet the Brooks and spent a few days enjoying the traditional tourist sites of London. We rented a car and drove through quaint English villages on our way to Cambridge. I wanted to see the university there, the ancient center of learning. In the late afternoon we sat in an ancient pew to pray. Evensong echoed throughout the halls of the Anglican Church of St. Mary the Great. We spent the night in a two-story, painted pink, B&B. The next morning we took an overnight train to Edinburgh. At five am. I stood in the train aisle looking out the window anticipating my first view of the homeland of my favorite historic but troubled monarch, Mary, Queen of Scots. The view from the train was rolling green moors speckled with hundreds of white sheep. The train tracks skirted the North Sea. That morning it was calm. It took all of ten minutes to realize I was finding my home away from home. I was awestruck by the wild beauty of the land, the hauntingly mysterious castle and tower ruins, and the cottages covered in bright red, blooming roses. The yellowest of all Scotland's flowers, Gorse, grew on every hill and lined walking paths across the countryside and in the Queen's Park in the heart of Edinburgh. With Frank as our guide, we absorbed his vast knowledge of church and Presbyterian history. Frank turned history into secular stories and funny episodes about folks like John Knox and the various husbands of Mary, the powerless and easily manipulated Queen of Scotland. He was gently leading Neil into a sacred space both externally and internally.

While in Edinburgh we took a taxi out to worship at Roslyn Chapel, seven miles from the city center. There were only eight of us at the service. Afterwards, we spent hours in the chapel marveling at the works of art on every wall, column, ceiling, and floor. There was a rumor that the Ark of the Covenant was buried under the chapel, but the Scottish government would not allow any excavation. The next day we walked our way through the city of Edinburgh where the Edinburgh Castle sits like a crown on a hill of solid rock. After hours of exploring the castle, I sat quietly on top of the castle in the tiny chapel of Queen Margaret while the others went to see the Crown Jewels. We strolled down the Royal Mile from the castle to Holyrood and toured the Palace where Mary's Italian secretary Rizzio was murdered by her second husband. In that same room was a framed piece of fabric on which Mary had attempted to stitch a scene. Never having used a needle in my life, it looked like something I might have done.

As we left the city and drove to Kinrosshire, I spied, half hidden by brush, the castle on an island in the middle of Loch Leven where Mary had been imprisoned and escaped in a laundry basket. Thoughts of her hardly left my consciousness.

In Kinrossshire we had to pass through an iron gate to reach Tulliebole Castle, where Lord and Lady Moncrieff and their son Roger would host us for one night. The 12th century castle had just recently been accepted as part of the Scottish Trust. Tulliebole had walls six feet thick, a door near the ceiling of the Great Room that went nowhere, and a fireplace so large a man could stand in it with plenty of head room. The Lord's name was Col. Harry Moncrieff. He had served in the War in India and still wore his patched elbowed jacket, sipped whiskey and petted his rather large hound while we all gathered round to make introductions. We were their first paying guests and they treated us as family. We ate dinner in their kitchen warmed by an open fire.

Frank asked the Lord what kind of fish we were eating and the Lord responded, "We are dining on poached fish."

He had fished illegally in Loch Leven.

We laughed at that and then laughed more when the Lord, out of politeness, asked Frank if he would like to say grace. Frank thought he had asked if Frank wanted a cigarette.

"No, thanks," Frank answered, "not while eating dinner."

The Lord looked amused.

That night, after climbing the curved concrete stairs, Neil and I entered our room. It was freezing. I pulled the sheet down off our bed and saw what looked like a moonshine jug. I thought the Lord had hidden some of his beloved whiskey in our bed. I removed it and found it warm. The next morning I learned it was a hot water bottle to warm our bed. We didn't need the jug; Neil and I warmed the bed ourselves.

After a breakfast of kippers and eggs, the Moncrieffs took us to Dollar, Scotland, to visit Castle Campbell, one of the best preserved castles in all of Scotland. John Knox hid in that castle to avoid treachery by the still reigning Catholics. To reach the castle we had to park the car and hike up a steep hill, cross over a running brook, then down the same steep hill. Each step captivated me and I did not want to leave. Ever. We picnicked in the rain on the side of a brook that fell like a waterfall, the mist covering us and our food. Mushy bread never tasted so good.

With great warmth of friendship we left Tulliebole and drove through the Cairngorm Mountains. Frank stopped the car long enough for three of us to take the ski lift to the top. Through clouds and mists and sunshine peeking through, Neil, JoAnn and I glimpsed miles and miles of the Cairngorms, ancient valleys, and snow still on the mountains' tops. The panoramic view was spellbinding. We were reluctant to leave.

At the Kyle of Lochalsh we spent the night at the Kyle Hotel and took the ferry to the Isle of Skye for a few hours of exploration. Then on to Oban that looked more like a beach in Florida than one on the west coast of Scotland. Early the next morning we took another ferry out to the island

Lord Moncrieff at Tulliebole Castle in Kinrossshire

of Mull. We waited over an hour, standing up, for a bus to come take us across the island. On the far shore we climbed into a 15-foot motor boat that delivered us, damp through and through, to the Isle of Iona which was for four hundred years a center of Celtic monasticism. There the Church of Scotland was rebuilding the chapel, turning it into a retreat center, and beginning to find and publish ancient Celtic chants, poems, psalms, and hymns. I was intrigued with the burial ground near the chapel which contained the body of the Scottish King Macbeth. I was astounded to see how short he was, based on the concrete sculpture atop the tomb.

When we returned to the mainland we drove down to Loch Ness and stopped to feel the mystery of its depths and howling winds. I wrote poems about Mull, Loch Leven and the Cairngorms. I read them aloud as we drove from village to village. My three traveling companions were great editors!

All too soon it was time to return to Gulfport. On the plane back home I cried like I was being torn from a part of me that was absolutely essential.

Neil was quiet and whispered to me, "We have just left a holy land."

• • •

Back at home, I realized I was pregnant. Our second son was born in February of 1967. He had been conceived in the cold bed at Tulliebole Castle in Kinrosshire, Scotland. When Frank Brooks talked about baptizing our new son, whom we had named "Harry" after my father, he suggested the middle name "Kinross." When we sent a photo of baby Harry to the Moncrieffs and told them he had been conceived in their castle, the Lord wrote us a letter telling us he had put our Harry's photo on the huge mantel in the great room. He wrote, "My lovely Lady and I are both proud for you. However, we do feel somewhat responsible!"

Harry Kinross White spent the major portion of his first two years of life in a playpen listening to music. Alma, our housekeeper, kept watch hoping Harry would soon be talking and walking. However, he seemed content to be outside most days, lolling in the playpen as long as the radio was turned to a music station. In the middle of his second year, he began to talk in sentences.

One day he cried, "I want to hear the bells."

None of us knew what he meant. This demand for bells went on for a week. One morning I was in the kitchen and heard Harry yelling, "The bells! The bells are here!"

The song playing was "Raindrops Keep Falling on My Head." In the background chimes were ringing. Harry heard what the rest of us had not.

13

When Neil's parents split up, his mother Martha moved to Poplarville, Mississippi. The Old Dog rented an apartment and began courting women of all ages.

Against the odds, these two had stayed married for nearly 30 years and produced six children, three boys and three girls. Three years before their divorce, they had been living in Bayou View in an expanded ranch house. The children — except for Margie who had married at age eighteen and moved away with her husband Bill — were still in school. Neil and I moved in to help take care of them.

Neil's younger brothers, George and Johnny, were excellent golfers and played nearly every afternoon after school. George also played the piano and guitar. He had a small band that practiced in the back of the house. His sister Hazel took ballet from Delia Stewart and she was a gifted dancer and choreographer. Martha, the youngest, had no guidance and no known interest. She occupied herself in creative ways like cutting her own hair and dying it with iodine.

George had a girlfriend. To be encouraging I asked him if he had ever kissed her.

"No," he said, "but I bit her on the leg once."

George also wrote a post card to a friend at Walloon Lake, Michigan. He went to the post office, asked for a stamp, and told the clerk to charge it to his mother.

That's how they lived. No money. Just charge accounts.

Living with the children, we did our best to keep their clothes clean and see that they got to school on time. We also had Neil III with us who adored his teenaged aunts and uncles. The seven of us spent many after-noons in the living room with George teaching little Neil how to sing a Bea-tles song. Hazel taught him how to do a *Tour jete*. Johnny and Martha danced with him, played ball with him, and rocked him to sleep.

Neil and I were in our mid-20s, living in a house with four teenagers and our own child. I realized we were in over our heads when we found out we had no control over their behavior. Hazel, an eighth grader, slipped out at night to meet a high school senior. I was up early one morning as Hazel was coming home at dawn in disheveled clothes. Often Johnny skipped school to play golf. Martha, in the sixth grade, found her mother's cigarettes and was teaching herself how to blow smoke rings.

They needed parental guidance that Neil and I were unprepared to provide. Admitting defeat, we sent some of them to stay with their dad for a while. The others went to Poplarville to live with their mother on a barge she had bought. She made a bar out of it. With a heart of gold she never sold a drink. She gave away the bar, then the barge, plus several other busi-nesses. She went bankrupt. Eventually Martha, once rolling in money, moved into a government housing complex called Rolling Hills. She worked as a sales clerk at Goodwill Industries.

• • •

During the years after he'd left Martha, Old Dog continued his shenanigans. He got involved with a few married women. Then he met a lady who was recently widowed. He asked her to marry him and she agreed. Two weeks later she was en route to Jackson to shop for clothes. Her energy ran out so she returned to Old Dog's house. She found her young daughter and Old Dog in bed together.   A few days later, she overdosed on pills.

Several months later, Old Dog married the daughter.

Since Old Dog lived next door to us, I agreed to arrange the wedding and reception for him and his bride. We all lived on the golf course so we decided to do the wedding in Old Dog's house which his fiancé had re-carpeted in all white.

She wore an orange dress and made a grand entrance from the garage. I planned for them to marry to the soft music on the FM station at 10:30 in the morning. The plan was that Judge Gaston Hewes would be fin-ishing his golf round at that time and would drop by to officiate.

Old Dog was clothed in a blue suit and a cold sweat. The judge's golf game ran over, so Old Dog and his bride were married to the 11 o'clock weather report.

They left right after the ceremony and went to New York City for their honeymoon.

14

On a rainy, winter day in January, 1969, I decided to stay inside to clean out my sons' clothing, toys, and books they no longer used. There were piles of items stacked in the hallway waiting to be sent to Goodwill.

The doorbell rang.

I was filthy and didn't want to see anyone, but the bell rang again.

I went to the front bedroom to look out the window. In the driveway was an old black car with a dented fender. I couldn't see who was at the door, so I walked to the foyer and looked out the window.

The Pastoress Eula Jones had returned. My thought was, "Oh, Lord, what now?"

I opened the door but did not invite her in.

"Mrs. Jane," she said, "I come with more information. The Good Holy Sovereign God told me to get myself over here to say to you, 'Do not doubt this prophecy,' and I knowed that's just what you been doing."

Reluctantly, I invited her in.

HuaHua, the Chihuahua, was still with her. I assumed they were not hungry since they didn't ask for hot dogs. Good thing. I had never replaced the hot dogs they'd consumed on their last visit. We walked to the den, and again she sat in the comfortable recliner. I sat on the brick hearth.

"Miss Eula," I said. "I don't mean any disrespect, but of course I doubt your prophecy. Speaking in tongues, twirling around like you're doing the Saint Vitus dance, is all unfamiliar to me. I don't know what else to do but doubt."

Shan de la caahh! she shouted. "Here's the deal. You remember the Bible story of Abraham?"

"Yes." I told her I'd read Genesis.

"Well, God promised Abraham a son and old Abraham was nigh unto one hundred years old before that promise, that prophecy came to pass. Now, God told me to get over here and tell you and your Mister he can't wait that long. The Lord God needs somebody to tell the truth about him right here and now! Mr. Neil White the Junior needs to get going on this here mission, and I mean, pronto."

"Miss Eula, you know I can't convince Neil to do anything at all. How am I supposed to encourage him to give up his law career to be a preacher?" I paused and added, "It's not just improbable . . . it's impossible."

"OOOHhh, watch yourself, Young Lady. Ain't nothing impossible with God. So here's what you do. You keep your mouth shut and pray. Me and God'll handle the rest."

"That's about all I can do, is be quiet, pray, and see what happens. All this talk of his becoming a preacher is foreign to me and to him. It's foolish to even consider it. He's not going to change."

"Well, now there are a few things to consider. There are all kinds of preacher men. Some choose them high-falutin' churches where preachers get free houses and cars and make some good money. But some of thems are charlatans. Then there's small churches where the preacher gets to know folks and they grow in the spirit together. Then there's what I do. Tent revivaling is good. You don't got no boss, no committee overseeing what you say and do, and Mr. Neil White the Junior might just like that about it. Here's the thing though. If he chooses tent revivaling you got to unpretty yourself a bit. Them men that come to the altar to confess might be getting lusty thoughts just looking at you instead of listening to the preacher's words. Yes, Ma'am. You just may need to put on some weight and cut that long red hair so wont no one want to touch it. Yep, that's what you got to do. My putting on weight done served my ministry well. Men don't much think lustily about me no more. Nope. They know they got to listen to me — not no looking at me."

I shook my head. "In my wildest imagination, I can not conjure up any image of Neil desiring to be a preacher at all, much less a tent evangelist!"

"Don't you be so sure!" she said, as she shook her finger at me.

She stood up, heisted HuaHua up into her arms and started toward the door.

Then she turned around and said, "I got an offer to make. I can come babysit your two boys anytime you need me. That way they'll get to know me better and I can work a bit on their souls while I'm at it."

Then Miss Eula threw her head back and shouted *Ooooo shan de la caaah!*

She handed me a sheet of paper. "My telephone number's on that there sheet. Don' lose it. You'll be calling me."

I thought, *Over my dead body will I be calling you to babysit my children.*

Weeks later, though, I did just that.

15

Education had been the focus of my mother's, my grandmother's, and my great-grandmother's lives, so naturally I believed they knew the right and wrong ways to teach a child. When Baby Neil, whom we now called Neil III, began school I observed with dismay the myriad ways in which his creativity, his questioning, was stifled. When he was in kindergarten I was told that Neil, III was *retarded* in coloring because he didn't stay within the lines. I informed the teacher that kindergarten children should not stay in lines because they are still in the exploration days and need not be limited in that way.

The next year, as a first grader in a local elementary school, Neil was repeatedly instructed not to laugh. This child was born thinking everything was funny. Joy bubbled up out of him. Time and time again his teachers sent notes home for me to please force Neil to be more serious and not ask so many questions in class.

That did it. I was not going to allow this precious child, this gift from God, to endure eleven more years of a stifling school experience. Determined to provide an exciting education for him, Mama and I talked about developing a private school where learning was fun, yet meaningful.

In early 1968, I was bedridden with the flu. As I lay in a pool of feverish sweat, a vision came to me. A school where a child was free to learn, free to be creative, free to explore and ask questions, free to become the individual he or she was destined to become. There would be discipline, of course, but it would be a discipline in which the child himself would participate.

I spent time in bed perfecting the motto: *Esse Quam Videri* meaning *"to be rather than to seem to be"*. I came up with the nickname *"The Crusaders"* for our sports teams. I asked my friend Jimmy Kennedy to design the logo.

The classes were not going to be first, second, third, etc., rather they would have names such as the Explorers, Apprentices, Masters. When I began to feel better, I called the State Department of Education to ask for information on creating a new but accredited school. Even though I had at that time a Master's Degree in Sociology, and a teaching certificate, I needed three other courses to be certified as a principal.

With my mother's support, nearly every week I spoke to civic groups and women's circles. I wrote articles for the paper expressing the need for a private school where all races were welcomed and the cost was only one dollar a day. It was the 1960s and it was crucial that people realize I was not starting this school to avoid integration. Just the opposite. This school would, from the beginning, be open to children of all races and be-liefs.

I took evening courses under Dr. Mercer Miller at the Keesler Air Force branch of the University of Southern Mississippi and received my certification as a principal.

For weeks my mother and I had concentrated on making plans for the new school we were developing. She was excited about writing plans, developing schedules, working up reading lists for each grade level, and writ-ing a school philosophy that expressed our desire to have every student love the learning process. As we worked closely together, I noticed Mama had a deep cough. I asked her if she had seen a doctor.

"No need to," she said, "It's just a bother."

We continued our plans day after day. Daddy and Harriet did not encourage us. They both expressed disdain.

"It won't work," they said. "There is no need for a private school.

Who will teach? Who will pay for it?"

Mama and I, so certain this school was part of God's plan for us, ignored them both.

After a few weeks, Mama's dresses seemed too big for her. Her cough persisted. I asked Daddy about it.

"She's just tired," he said. Then he added, "You are putting too much pressure on her about this school idea."

Later that day, I pleaded with Mama to call Dr. Culler, our family physician, for an appointment. I went with her to see him. After her examination, Dr. Culler said, "I am recommending Elizabeth see a doctor at Ochsner's Hospital in New Orleans.

"What's wrong?" I asked.

"I'm not certain," he said, "but I don't like the cough and the weight loss. Let's see what Ochsner's tells us."

The next week, Daddy took off from work and drove Mama to the hospital. After the tests, the doctor at Ochsner's insisted that Mama be admitted. They wanted to remove some lymph nodes and send them to the lab. Daddy called to say he was going to stay over at the Brent House until the lab results came back.

It was a Wednesday afternoon in early April. A spring day. Flowers were blooming. A breeze off the gulf cooled the air. When the phone rang, I leapt for it. It was Daddy.

"Janie, the news is not good," he said. "I've called Dr. Culler and he is going to come by your house later today to talk to you. Your mama will be in the hospital for a few days and I am staying with her. Then we will be home."

I couldn't take a deep breath. For something to be wrong with my mother was not an option. Life, my life, depended on her, her encouragement, her love, and her confidence in me. She had to get well. Whatever it took she would be well. I waited on the porch for Dr. Culler. My obsession with my mama's health consumed me.

Dr. Culler arrived. I invited him into the house.

"No," he said, "let's visit out here."

"What's wrong with Mama?"

"Jane, the diagnosis is she has lymphatic carcinoma."

"What does that mean?"

"It's cancer. It has moved through her body by way of lymph glands."

"What medicine or treatment will make her well?"

He hesitated. "There is not much that can be done. There is a slight possibility that cobalt treatments may lessen the spread."

"Well, let's do that. When can she start the treatments?"

"There is a cobalt machine at the Biloxi hospital. If your mother is willing I will set it up. But you must understand this treatment is a long shot. Cobalt burns the inside of the body and makes the person quite ill."

"She's already ill. Won't this help?"

"Let's talk to your mother and see what she wants to do. Jane, I'm so sorry. Your mother is a grand lady, and an icon in this community. But cancer is not a respecter of persons. She will suffer, and so will you."

From that moment on my life changed in ways I never anticipated. I lived in fear twenty-four hours a day. I could not sleep for the thoughts that plagued me. I begged Mama to take the cobalt treatments.

Daddy said, "We will do only what your mother wants to do. If she chooses the treatments you will have to take her. I have to go back to work."

"Of course I'll take her," I said.

And I did. Every other day for six weeks we drove to the hospital in Biloxi. I helped her down the sloping walkway to the basement. The monstrous machine took up a large portion of the room. It reminded me of a medieval torture machine. As it turned out, that was an apt description.

Each day as we returned home from Biloxi, Mama would struggle to walk to the back bedroom, then hurry to the bathroom to vomit up her charred and burned insides. She gasped for breath between each upheaval. I had to go in and hold her body while it seemed her life was being emptied into the toilet. I was desperate for any distraction.

Trying to act and be normal, Neil and I continued to attend spontaneous gatherings or parties that his group of young lawyers arranged almost every Friday or Saturday night. Some of the attorneys had a band of guitar, piano players, and singers. The music was fun, uplifting, and nostalgic. One of the band members paid attention to me. He sought me out at each break, sat beside me, and talked. He told me ideas he had about the universe and how his mother thought the trip to the moon by our astronauts did not happen.

"They filmed it in Arizona," he said.

He shared titles of books he read, ones he thought I might like. He offered to give them to me. He shared his childhood years about growing up outside of Poplarville in the back woods of Mississippi. His home was a tar paper shack with newspapers taped to the walls for insulation. These were different conversations from the others in the room.

The others, as far as I could tell, were mainly old jokes between co-workers, or the latest news about other friends and acquaintances. There were also serious rumors that everyone surreptitiously listened to. And always about exciting cases these young, aspiring attorneys were handling. While my friend and I talked, I did not think about my mother.

Daddy and Vi were so eager to give Mama hope, they bought her the new house two doors down from Neil and me. She was as delighted as she could be in her state. Her moving close to me allowed me to spend more time with her. During the days I sat with her. I tried to interest her in the progress I was making with our new school we were setting up in the fellowship hall of Westminster Church. She smiled when I talked about Neil and Harry, or when I brought them over to see her. Most of the time she listened to me chatter on and on. I was distracting myself so I would not think about her illness. Mama seldom responded. Except one afternoon, she asked me to sit next to her. She reached out for my hands. Her voice was weak.

"Janie, I love you. I do not want to leave you. But I am not going to get well."

It was a death sentence not just for her but for me as well. Life became all about me and my mental, emotional, and spiritual survival.

"Mama you have to get well. I cannot live without you. You are young, only 56 years old! You have years ahead of you. I can't live without you."

"On the contrary," she whispered. "You will live more expansively without me. In fact, my passing will set you free to be you…your beautiful, compassionate, loving self."

I put my head in her lap and cried until there were no more tears. When I could stand up, I helped Mama get back to her room and in the bed. I covered her up and kissed her on her forehead. It was damp and warm. I wondered how many more times I would be able to touch her, hug her, be near her.

I walked home. Neil was at work. Alma was watching Harry. Neil III was on his bike riding around Southern Circle with his friends. I took down a phone book, looked up the number of a law office, and called my new singing friend. The one who I thought would save me.

I also called Miss Eula. When she answered the phone, I told her about my mother's illness. I spoke more loudly than I intended. "Where is your God when I need Him? What about your prophecy? It's all a lie! I'm hurting and don't know what to do."

I was choking on my tears.

Miss Eula replied, "Jane, I told you before to keep your mouth shut and pray. It is time for you to learn to trust God Almighty. I know you say you love the Lord, but I don't think you even know how to trust Him with the lives of the people you love. You gotta change that, girl, or you'll never ever have any peace."

I hung up on her.

The weaker Mama got, the more often I called the law office. Or at his invitation, visited him there under the pretense of his doing some legal work for me. His laughter and absurd stories amused me. For brief moments in time my grief subsided. His antics made me forget my mother was dying, hour by hour.

On July 4, 1968, Mama went into a coma. The ambulance came to take her to the hospital. Daddy stood in their front yard with tears pouring down his face, wetting his collar and shirt front. I tried to put my arms around him, but he moved away and said, "Don't. Don't touch me, or I may fall apart."

Standing only two feet apart we cried out our separate griefs, and watched the ambulance leave with Mama inside. She stayed in the hospital. Daddy kept watch beside her every morning then worked in the afternoons. I drove to the hospital every afternoon to sit with Mama. I held her hand, told her what progress the school we named Westminster Academy was making, that I had purchased the tables and chairs, the wall posters, and many books. I reassured her that no matter what the school would open on August 25, just like we had planned. Mama never once regained consciousness. Dr. Culler told me to keep talking to her. She could possibly hear me, but could not respond. I talked for hours every afternoon, not wanting to break that fragile connection with her.

When I left the hospital each afternoon, I stopped by the wall of payphones in the lobby to make a call. Talking to my friend was an addiction and a fix. I needed to find the courage to go home, mother my little boys, and try to be the wife Neil expected. My man friend and my family were obsessions that vied with each other for my attention. I felt my sanity slipping away.

One day when I left the hospital later than usual, I walked out to the parking lot. My friend was there parked next to me. I sat in his front seat beside him. He took my hand. "Hey, Pretty Girl, I'm too smitten with you. It isn't right. You know it and I know it. What are we going to do?"

I didn't reply.

He said, "If I could change it all for you I would do it. I don't have that power. What I can do is love you from afar and let go of this friendship.

"Right now," I said, "I need you. You make me forget my mother is dying. Please, wait."

"Ok, but if Neil finds out our lives will never be the same."

I left him and drove up and down the beach for an hour. When I finally returned home Neil asked me where I had been.

"Thinking," I said. Then I blurted out, "Neil, I am not happy with us. I want some time away from you to think, sort out who I am and what I want."

"You have everything anybody could want. A husband who loves you, two little boys, and a job you have been craving! What's the matter, are you crazy?"

He called Dr. Wilson, a psychiatrist who treated his mother and aunt.

Dr. Wilson asked me to check into the hospital so he could treat me daily. I refused. My mother had suffered so much. I couldn't stand to be in the hospital another minute.

"I can arrange for a room at Driftwood Nursing Home," he said.

Again, I refused.

"You can do this voluntarily," he said, "or we can use legal means."

I was too exhausted to fight.

I went to Driftwood. They took my clothes, my purse, my money, and the Bible I always had in my purse. I wasn't allowed visitors except Daddy and my aunt Vi.

When they came to see me, they expressed concern about Mama, my boys, and me, yet they had no solutions to my despair. Every day I was fed five tiny meals of mushed up vegetables, potatoes, and served hot chocolate at night to help me sleep. I had a daily therapy session with Dr. Wilson.

He asked me again and again, "What are you running toward? Where do you want to be and what do you want to do? Who do you want to be? Do you want to be a wife or a mistress?"

"It's not like that, Dr. Wilson. It isn't really an affair. It's a friendship that helps me laugh and endure my misery. That's all."

"Well, Neil calls it an affair," Dr. Wilson said, "and I agree with him."

"Of course you do." I felt trapped. "Right now, I just want to go home, hold my boys, and get some rest."

After four days, I did go home. I tried to pay more attention to my family, my daddy who was also miserable, and still find time to stay with Mama at the hospital, and finish the preparation for the new academy. At least at night I was tired enough to sleep.

August 15 was Neil's and my wedding anniversary. We went out to dinner and tried to be less prickly with each other. We talked mainly about Neil III and Harry.

The next day, Sunday, August 16, 1968, my mother died. I survived the funeral and burial by smiling, laughing, talking too loud, and pretending I was someone else.

This was not my mother, but a stranger, I told myself. *I was no longer Jane. I was a different person, a less caring, a less feeling person.*

As promised, I opened Westminster Academy on August 25 with a full staff of creative teachers and five full classrooms of fifteen students each. In my mind, Westminster Academy became a living memorial to my mother.

Neil did try to comfort me. He offered to be more involved in our church, in the academy, in the lives of our boys. He became a coach for our school's football team. He was elected an elder in the church and later elected the church treasurer. He seemed to take his responsibilities more seriously. His efforts had little effect on me, except when I pretended they did.

A month into being the principal of Westminster Academy, a flower arrangement was delivered to my office. The card said, "Keep your chin up. I am closer than you think."

I threw away the card, vowing I would not pick up the phone to call him. A week later, I was in Jones Brothers Drug Store. My admirer was at the checkout counter. When I saw him, I felt lighter. I smiled, making my face feel less tight. I walked over to him. He saw me, reached out, took my hand, and asked, "How are you?"

"I am not. I don't exist," I replied.

"Come with me to my apartment and let's talk," he said.

I followed him, went in, and sat at his kitchen table. As we talked I realized just how emotionally involved I was with him. And more, I realized emotional involvement was far more seductive than a physical relationship could possibly be. He urged me to tell him about my mother. I did. I talked for nearly an hour. As I did, it was like the museum of her I carried on my back felt lighter. We laughed. He sang to me. Standing by his kitchen stove with dishes piled up in his sink, we kissed and embraced. I felt attached. Less isolated.

Driving home, the Museum of Mama Memories morphed into a gallery of guilt. I could not live two lives. Hiding myself no longer had an appeal. An appeal that had gripped me for most of my life. I wanted to be openly and authentically me. I didn't want to be Elizabeth's daughter, Floy's granddaughter, Harriet's sister, ethical Harry Stanley's child. I wanted to be me. But that was a journey I did not know how to begin.

My mother and I had worked together for months to make sure we had every aspect of the school planned out, ready to implement. The school was to be a living memorial not only to her but also to my grandmother Floy. Tragically, I opened the school without my mother. Two weeks after her death. With the reputations of Mama and Floy behind me, Westminster Academy opened fully accredited in the fall of 1968. I became its principal.

I hired teachers (for the most part mothers of our students) — Dale Simpkins, Patricia Weatherly, Willadora Kremer, Betsy Douglas, Karen Waller, Barbara Cunningham, Edie Kennedy, and Marcia Taylor. They were superb, creative teachers. I wrote a theme based curricula for all the grades and encouraged parental involvement. I planned to take students on field trips to New Orleans and Mobile to experience the French, Arcadian and Spanish influences in houses, buildings, cathedrals, iron grill work, and food.

Neil's grandmother Ritchie had purchased the largest organ on the coast for Westminster Presbyterian Church. His uncle Knox had donated the pulpit and choir stalls. Their generosity helped make Westminster one of the most beautiful churches in Gulfport. And husband Neil was on the board of elders.

With his support, along with the support of Sherwood Bailey, Chunn Sneed, Cleve Allen, Helen Walker, Paul Wright, Bill Petty, Jimmy Kennedy, Roland Weeks and Stella Hemphill, I gained approval to utilize the Westminster church facilities for the first year of school. Additionally, Jack Thompson came on board as did Harry Simpkins. The Sunday School rooms became school rooms Monday through Friday. We started each school day in the chapel with singing and prayers.

We had a Pee Wee football team coached by John McCurdy, Oney Raines and my husband. We rarely won a game, but our little boys played with heart.

We tried new and creative activities in every class. Some of them worked; some did not. We were crowded and cramped. In a particularly in-

Me with Westminster students outside the Apprentice classroom

spired moment at Shoney's Restaurant, I sketched on the back of a paper napkin the kind of school facility I dreamed of: a great room for collective activities, each classroom having its own door to the outside. Jimmy Kennedy and Arvah McLendon took those ideas and designed the first building.

Of course, we had no land.

To remedy that situation, I went to Mayor Billy Meadows to ask if I could purchase the open ditch behind Westminster Presbyterian Church. It was a wide ditch allowing rainwater to drain from the Bayou View area. The church was adjacent to a six acre park which we had access to in order to qualify for accreditation. To be accredited the school had to have access to a green-space play area. Mayor Meadows asked why I wanted the ditch and I explained that we needed to build a school building on it because we were outgrowing the church's facilities. He contacted the two city commissioners and with a smile on his face he asked how much I intended to pay for the ditch. I opened my wallet which had a $10 bill in it and handed it across the desk to him. We received the deed to the property. Less than three weeks later I was back in his office asking the city to put a culvert in the ditch and cover it with dirt so we could begin our building. They did. And we did.

The academy buildings were constructed on top of that filled in ditch.

To me, it was fitting. Important things can be built from nothing.

The visions I had for Westminster Academy came from my mother's and grandmother's teaching philosophies — and my own experiences. I had taught Sociology at Gulf Park College and could tell almost immediately which students had experienced "good" elementary school teaching because it affected their attitudes toward learning, their ability to learn and study, and their general comfort within their own intelligence. I also enjoyed such tidbits of information about how the word "academy" came to be. Plato's best friend was named Academus. Together these two young men sat in Academus' garden perched on a hilltop overlooking the city of Athens. As these two curious and well-instructed men talked about the known world and their thoughts about history, language, geography, and literature, they looked down at the masses in the city and agreed that these people, too, needed a way to talk about things aside from their daily survival. As a result, these two men began to invite butchers, blacksmiths, fishmongers, and laborers to attend some discussion sessions. Thus, the first university or "academy" was born, fittingly named for Academus.

I liked the idea of blending different ages and interests together, so that first year at Westminster we had many community guests come in to share their knowledge with us. Dr. Richard Buckley, my friend Tish's husband, a neurosurgeon, came to teach us about the brain. George Schloegel, the same Georgie of my childhood, spent time discussing banking and numbers to our classes. Roland Weeks shared his ideas about journalism and publishing newspapers. Shep Crigler came and discussed aspects of church history. Mrs. Floyd taught us about birds and bird-watching. Bill Hainey worked his magic and helped establish a library by having McGraw-Hill share with us their extra books. We took field trips to the library, the harbor, and local industries; afterwards the students came back and shared creatively what they had learned.

It was a fun, exciting and stimulating time, yet it was darkened by the death of my mother. Not only was she to have managed the school with me, she had been for years the most exciting person I knew. My mother, the star of the drama of my early life, was gone.

Neil Jr. and John McCurdy at Westminster football practice

16

Neil and I committed to become more active in Westminster Presbyterian Church.

Through the love and support we found at Westminster, especially from Frank and JoAnn Brooks, we both felt the missing piece to our relationship puzzle was in place. Certain the "answer to life" was the church, Neil left his law practice and planned to move us to Edinburgh, Scotland. He would become a minister and study at the Church of Scotland's New College Seminary.

Neil's spiritual conversion and decision to relocate us forced me to leave Westminster Academy in the hands of others. This loss, along with the loss of my mother and pending move to a country I'd only visited once, was daunting. But it was also exciting.

Our son Neil was old enough to be likewise excited and a bit fearful. Three-year-old Harry did not understand what was happening.

The week before we boarded the flight to Scotland, there was a brief article in the local newspaper about us.

"The young Whites, on their unselfish way to be part of saving the world, remind me of an ancient wise man, Diogenes. He owned one possession: a wooden bowl. He carried this possession with him always. From this bowl he ate his daily meal of oats, drank his water and ale and used it as a pillow on which to rest his head during nightly sleeps. One day, he dropped his possession. As it broke in half, Diogenes exclaimed with relief, 'Ah, at last I am free.' How brave are Neil and Jane to give away all their earthly possessions and take abroad with them only their two little boys and three duffle bags of

personal items. Perhaps they are the hope we have all been waiting for. We wish them well."

I felt embarrassed. "If only they knew the truth," I thought.

Eager to leave and dispense with the unending questions of *Are you sure? Don't you want to wait a while?* and *Neil is a new Christian, maybe you ought to go to seminary closer home*, I kept my head down to hasten the time to leave. I needed a new life!

Frank called Neil and asked him to do the sermon at Westminster the Sunday before we left. Neil was hesitant, but agreed.

"Nothing like getting started early," he said.

Westminster Church was crowded that spring morning. Whispers of anticipation ran up and down the pews while organ music filled the sanctuary. The morning sun shining through the stained glass windows cast a blue hue across the chancel and the pulpit. At the stroke of 10 am, the acolytes entered, lighted the candles, and stood aside as the Reverend Frank Brooks in full ecclesiastical garb walked in ahead of the choir. Neil and I with son Neil sat on the second pew. When Frank walked by he nodded and smiled at Neil, surreptitiously giving him a thumbs up.

Some of the people in the congregation had heard we were moving away. Neil had given up his lucrative law practice and sold his car to Bill Rainey, a law associate. I had spent days giving away our worldly goods: furniture to friends, books to schools and the library, clothes to the Salvation Army and over 400 of our wedding gifts such as sterling silver trivets, serving dishes, tea and coffee sets, bread trays, engraved serving trays, and a table setting for 12 of Melrose sterling tableware to a church where Alma, our house keeper, worshipped. At the Army Surplus Store I had purchased two large duffel bags. One bag held our boys' clothes, heavy winter coats, a few toys, a special blanket for Harry, and a football for son Neil. In the other duffel I stuffed our clothes and two books, a Bible and a book *One Hundred of the World's Best Poems.*

We were ready.

Neil was nervous as he climbed the steps to the lectern. He stood still, opened his notes, straightened his tie, pushed his glasses further up his nose, and began by thanking Frank, Jo Ann and the congregation for their friendship, support, and encouragement.

He said, "I have made a decision that was not easy, but I think, and I hope, it is the right decision. I believe, as much as any of us can, that God spoke to me. I experienced a strong urge to leave the law and learn how to minister on God's behalf. Heaven knows if He has asked me, then *anyone* will do! Please, each of you, pray for me and for my family as we make our way to one of the oldest seminaries in the world, New College Seminary in Edinburgh, Scotland."

There were several audible gasps from the congregation.

Neil continued, "You see, New College was built in the 1500's so it is newer than the old one built in the 1300's. This ancient college is located on the Mound in Edinburgh, in the shadow of Edinburgh Castle's terrace. From the high steps of the seminary you can see the city in its entirety; that is the new city of Edinburgh along Princess Street." He paused, his lips trembled. He wiped his eyes. Looking down at his notes he said, "I'm rather new myself, at least to this business of God."

He stopped staring at his notes and looked directly out at the congregation, seeming to go row by row, pew by pew, nodding his head. In a courtroom style of voice he began his sermon with these words, "If religion is anything it has to be more than Bible, more than church, more than theology, more than denominations, and altogether more about love of God, self and others. And, I beseechingly pray it is specifically more about hope and faith, enough to help us abide in a world of hate and disappointment."

He spoke for 15 minutes. After his opening sentences I sobbed. I don't remember other specific words or sentences but I heard in his voice truth and courage, despair and hope. His once familiar voice sounded strange at this moment and in this place.

I wondered, "Is this my Neil speaking, or is it a new Neil under reconstruction? Were we running toward a new life, or were we escaping our old ones where hurt and blame and drunkenness and affairs had happened? If we were escaping then Neil needed a viable reason and God was apparently it."

When Neil left the lectern he came and sat down by me. He did not look at me, but he patted my knee.

I whispered to him, "You are wonderful. I'm so proud."

I noticed our son Neil put his small hand in his dad's larger one and squeezed.

During coffee time nearly every person stayed to speak to Neil, to encourage him, to offer prayers. They hugged me and young Neil, too. Harry came from the nursery, cookies in hand, and stood by his dad wrapping his free hand around Neil's pants' leg. Frank never left Neil's side. Frank was concerned about the abruptness of Neil's decision, yet he was supportive and loving.

People at the service that morning talked about Neil's sermon for years. Some still do. Each seemed deeply touched, perhaps by the words Neil spoke, but maybe more so by the audacity of Neil's decision. In 1969 in Gulfport, Mississippi, people just didn't give up work, leave family, home, and a comfortable lifestyle to move far away for God!

But we did.

• • •

The following week, when Neil's ex-law partner Bill Rainey came to pick us up to take us to the airport, he threw our duffle bags in the back of his station wagon. Neil III tightly clung to my daddy and Harry cried on Harriet's shoulder. Pulling them away, we scooted in the back seat with Neil III between us and Harry on my lap. I looked at my daddy and Harriet standing in the driveway watching us back away. Their ashen faces bore the skeletal looks of the forlorn and forgotten.

I told myself and my friends that our adventure crossing the ocean, leaving all that we knew behind, was to embrace a new life. But deep inside, I knew better. It was an attempt to run away from our previous one.

And it was one more place for me to continue to hide.

As we turned the corner on Southern Circle, we passed our former home where the tent-revivalist Eula Jones had paid me a visit three years earlier.

It seemed her prophecy was coming to pass.

17

We rented a flat at 5 Nile Grove in the Morningside district of Edinburgh, Scotland. The Scottish row houses on Nile Grove were dull beige except for the doors. They were painted bright red or blue.

My life felt like a monochrome of guilt. The red door at our flat reminded me every day of my adultery. Behind it our family of four lived.

Neil rode the Number 5 bus to the Mound where New College Seminary has stood for 600 years.

Neil III enrolled in fourth grade at Morningside School. The school lagged behind the U.S. in math and science (his mathematics book was entitled Sums — he'd already dabbled in algebra at Westminster Academy). But the curriculum in the humanities was light years ahead of the Americas. He studied Greek Mythology, World History, and the finer details of sentence diagramming. But his favorite activity was eating vanilla pudding in the cafeteria. He played rugby and soccer after school, and in the fall and winter he walked home in the dark at 4:00 pm wearing orange light reflectors on his arms.

Neil III, although only nine years old, figured out the money exchange rate before the rest of us. He volunteered to shop at the Green Grocer, the Fruiter-Florist, the Iron Monger, the Fish Monger and the bakery that specialized in strawberry tarts and lemon squares.

We had the good fortune of meeting another young American couple, Jim and Pat Fennel. They were from Alabama, and Jim, like Neil, was a wealthy, somewhat self-centered, charming southern gentlemen.

At our flat at 5 Nile Grove in Edinburgh

Pat and I recognized each other as kindred spirits and became fast friends.

Three-year-old Harry attended a half-day playschool at the Braid Church next door to our flat. He ate "elevensies," discovered that a cookie was a called a biscuit, and was told by his teacher he was a "cheeky thing."

In the afternoons, Harry and I explored Edinburgh with my new friend Pat. We picnicked in the Princess Street Gardens and shopped for anoraks and wool scarves at Marks & Spencer's. We ate watercress sandwiches on the fifth floor of Jenner's Department Store and bought artwork down the hill at Dean Village. We strolled down the Royal Mile from the Castle to Holyrood Palace, stopping to browse at antique stores and having afternoon crème teas at scone shops.

We were on the lookout for hamburgers, that elusive American delight that had not yet reached the shores of Scotland. To our relief we found a fast food restaurant called Wimpy's advertising an American hot dog. We rushed in, bought three, and discovered it was nothing more than a sausage sliced to curve and placed on a round bun.

On many of our excursions I dressed Neil and Harry in kilts. I wanted us to be a part — as well as dress the part — of Scotland. Neil III was quick to point out that none of the other Scottish kids his age were wearing kilts, but he sometimes acquiesced to please me and wore the kilt in spite of enduring some teasing from neighborhood children.

Neil entered New College Seminary with such hope and enthusiasm. But soon he discovered the vast academic ocean of theology was nothing like the pond of love we had discovered back at our Westminster Church.

The passion and calling that brought Neil to God were being distilled into homework assignments. He was being graded on challenging courses, not on his spiritual life.

Despair became his constant companion. I saw the weight of seminary's demands — and my indiscretions — crushing him. He escaped his sadness by drinking.

But there were still moments, glimpses really, of the man I fell in love with.

"Hey," he said at tea one night as I prepared a piece of toast, "you know the bible says we can't live by bread alone, so how 'bout putting some of that Norwegian butter and jam on it."

While Neil struggled to turn the intellectualism of Barth and the doctrines of Calvin and Knox into the soul nourishment he desperately wanted, I fell in love.

Scotland seduced me.

I studied, obsessed over, really, the history of the Protestant revolt; of Mary, Queen of Scots, and those who betrayed her; and of the sacred, inconsistent land itself. I read and read and read.

Then I journeyed to those sacred places, usually with Neil III and Harry in tow.

I knelt, filled with awe, in moldy, flag-filled St. Giles Cathedral on the Royal Mile. There I hungered to feel the presence of the Queen's spirit.

I prayed to forgive John Knox, that *arrogant bastard!* He persecuted my heroine — Mary — calling her "a bitch and a pawn of the satanic pope."

The crumbling tower of Linlithgow Palace cast a gray green shadow on the gravel drive. I climbed out of the car, leaned against it, and stared in awe at the birthplace of the victimized Mary, Queen of Scots. The low-ceilinged, arched entrance tunnel was paved with slabs of slate. Passing through the tunnel, I breathed the ageless dampness of the moldy bricks. I stepped straight through to the open courtyard. A familiar three-tiered waterless fountain stood like a sentinel in its midst. Walking through a chilled falling mist, I stopped. Startled by a certainty I had been in this place before. Centuries ago.

I felt the Queen's spirit surround me. Envisioning the three floors of the palace, the tapestries that once hung on icy walls, I entered the palace's

Great Room. There, on the hearth of the over-sized fireplace, sat the four hundred year old victim herself. My previous self.

A month later at a museum, an elderly docent saw me.

"Wait right here, Madam," she said, "I have something to show you."

Certain she had mistaken me for someone else, I moved through the aisles. The docent caught up with me, an ancient box in her hands. She placed the box on a glass topped counter, whipped out a headpiece, and placed it on my head.

"What are you doing?" I asked her.

"Oh, M'Lady, when you walked in, I knew immediately you were Queen Marie herself."

I stood awkwardly with the antique headdress sitting atop my red hair.

"I just had to see it," she said. "You know, sitting atop her red head." She looked me directly in the eye. "You are her very person, reincarnated."

• • •

Lately, I'd felt like I had been in Scotland centuries before — somehow, some way, at some time.

I dug my hands in the eons old dirt and sat on moss covered rocky shores begging salty waves to share their secrets. I saw the tumultuous land, its peoples' desperation for freedom, and longed for redemption.

Hoping to absorb the dampness of the muddy moors, I rolled my body down the bumpy slopes of Arthur's Seat in the Queen's Park. My ear to the ground, I heard centuries of tromping boots and bare feet living through hell to find an earthly heaven. My mind overflowed with visions of the gore and glory of the Scots' oppression rising to enlightenment, of their bodies and minds being set free from the confines of traditions mired in ignorance and complacency. It was everything Mary, Queen of Scots, desired.

And I believed with all my heart that the elderly docent had provided me with a connection to her, however improbable.

I felt a true kinship with that long ago misunderstood and mistreated Queen. I discovered we had much in common: She was tall and redheaded. She was not domestic. She loved horses. She had an affinity for husbands who did not suit her, nor her them. No one believed her either.

In December of 1969, three months pregnant with our third child, my husband of 10 years admitted defeat. He took a giant step of courage and dropped out of seminary.

We both cried. Then Neil retreated. Isolated.

That night after the children went to sleep, I walked outside in our neighborhood.

I sat on the wet curb of the street and shivered until all the guilt within me poured out of my nose and eyes and trembling lips. My life was in limbo, and I knew with clarity all of it was my fault.

18

Despite the difficulties in my relationship with Neil, in some ways my adult spiritual awakening began in Edinburgh. There I fell in love with everything I had not yet known.

As I walked though ancient castles, my body felt a connection with each one. The greater the history and disrepair, the more I *knew* it.

I rejoiced in finding standing stones out in rocky pastures or hidden on top of hills covered with golden rape. I wrapped my arms around the ancient monoliths hoping I could grasp their meanings. I crawled through the decaying dovecots listening for echoes of chirps that once meant there would be food for another day.

In Edinburgh, Pat and I attended evening lay classes taught by Professor James Stuart, the Queen's own Chaplain. Through his love of God and openness to faith in any form, I began to understand that Baptist dogma did not support freedom of spirit or thought. For me it confined God, limited love, and through threats of eternal hell, controlled behavior.

In Edinburgh, for the first time, I felt a spiritual freedom beginning to blossom. In my early Baptist days, those of us in the pews heard about the divinely Anglo-Saxon Jesus, never the thoroughly human, Jewish one who was a wild rebel, defying and moving beyond the laws and limitations of his own beloved, yet misunderstood, religion.

Here, I discovered the Baptist teachings of my youth were not factual. Biblical stories were not literally true.

Allegorically, they were true. . . or pointed to truth.

I had always sensed that Jesus was not born of a virgin. I doubted Jesus had actually walked on water. Rather his disciples knew him to be someone who could help them rise above their own normal confines and move into a life of meaning and worth. They used the words of fishermen to proclaim what Jesus meant to them, as well as to recount their personal enlightenment.

Professor Stuart taught us it was Saul/Paul who changed the religion *of* Jesus to a religion *about* Jesus. Jesus' religion was a way to live every day full of love, compassion, and forgiveness. Paul's religion about Jesus was formed by doctrine, dogma, and creedal beliefs. Dogma, doctrine, and creeds were necessary, baby steps toward wholeness, never a *fait accompli*.

My mind exploded with excitement.

I realized I could enjoy the colorful church rituals and traditions that have been kept alive for thousands of years without succumbing to the untruths and misunderstandings so many of them represented. I could honor those traditions as long as I knew the truth, lived the truth, and continued to seek other revelations regarding truth.

I promised myself I would stay free. Free to change my mind as I grew in knowledge, spirit, and, hopefully, wisdom.

Perhaps this was why we had come to Scotland.

For *me* to be inspired by the stories of the Scot's desiring freedom above all. While there, I read parts of the Arbroath Declaration that speaks of freedom being the only road to peace and tolerance.

It was there, in Scotland, where I learned freedom is costly — something or someone usually must die to have it.

I began to kill off the stifling aspects of institutionalized religion and I knew for the first time, the great gulf between religion and spirit was clear. I saw with great contrast the difference between doctrine and faith.

I finally understood that truth; only truth would set me free.

And I realized love can never be coerced. Forgiveness can never be

On windy Blackford Hills in Edinburgh

given by someone for someone else.

It is all — every bit of it — personal.

I stood on top of wind-whipped Blackford Hills. I had a panoramic view of Edinburgh and the North Sea. As I looked toward Princess Street Gardens, the Pentland Hills, Castle Rock, and the spires of New College Seminary, my mind reeled with the unthinkable.

Was it possible that Eula Jones' prophecy was not quite accurate?

Was it possible that I, not Neil, was the one who was destined for ministry?

19

In May of 1970, we left Edinburgh. We moved back home to Gulfport. On the plane ride back to the United States, Neil III, who had just turned ten, asked his dad about leaving seminary.

"What if somebody asks why you aren't a preacher?"

My husband thought for a moment. Then he answered, "Just tell them I cussed too much."

• • •

Three weeks after we arrived our third child was born. Elizabeth Jane (Liz), our only daughter, arrived June 12, 1970. We hoped the newness of her life would somehow spread into our own.

Since Neil had not worked in a year, we had little money. My dad bought us a used car. Aunt Vi bought a two-bedroom house for us for $17,000.00. We were grateful, but at the moment had no way to repay the expenses.

Neil started going out, drinking heavily. He was away from home night after night.

I memorized the phone numbers of all his favorite hangouts and most of the bars from Biloxi to Long Beach. Many a night I called just to ask if Neil was there and if he was okay.

In the late hours of the night, I sat on our front stoop hoping and

Liz and me (above) in 1972
Jamie and me (below) in 1973

waiting to hear the sound of his car turning the corner. From lack of sleep, fear, and no appetite, I lost 30 pounds. Once again, I had a waist.

Neil opened his private law practice in the Hewes Building in downtown Gulfport. At first there were not many clients. Our days together were difficult.

We saw counselors. One in New Orleans. On one of the trips, we decided to stay overnight in hopes of rekindling some kind of romance. We had Trout Almondine by candlelight at Arnaud's then went to the Monteleone Hotel.

Nine months later our fourth child Walter James (Jamie) was born. I slept on the couch with Jamie on my stomach for the first months of his life. His warmth, the sweet aroma of baby shampoo, and his chubby hands holding firmly onto my thumbs, offered me a peace I found nowhere else.

My four babies — and my intense love and need for them — filled me with happiness.

This joy, this innocent love, did not repair the damage to my marriage. Neil became more and more angry. We kept our distance from each other.

A struggling law practice provided few funds. Westminster Academy was running smoothly without me, so I was content to let it be.

I knew we needed additional income, but I also needed someone at home to tend to the babies, clean the house, and fix supper.

I re-hired Alma Savoy, a happy-go-lucky woman who stood no more than 4' 10" tall. I promised her we would share equally in whatever monthly check I received.

I took a job as a first grade teacher to 36 children at North Gulfport Elementary School. Many of the children did not know their last names. Although the Civil Rights Act of 1964 had been passed eight years earlier, the school was still all-black and located in one of the most impoverished areas of the Gulf Coast.

The five acres of school ground were barren. Only a few scraggly shrubs and a few hundred small, black feet broke the monotony of white, sandy soil. There were no shade trees. The only tint in the vast mono-color of building and yard was the faded flag waving high over the entrance. Weathered trash blew against the concrete foundation of the building.

My classroom was large and dirty. The table and desks were clustered together at the front of the room leaving a back area open. In the far corner was a small bathroom that had a tiny sink and toilet. The bathroom was a favorite of all the children, partly because of its novelty. Most of the children didn't have indoor plumbing.

I was the only white teacher in the school.

My first week at work the teacher across the hall from my classroom sent me a note:

Roses are red, students are black.
Curtis Lee got ringworm all over his back.

I knew I was in for a long year.

The first day on the job I learned a few facts. No child in the classroom could read. Most thought the state in which they lived was North Gulfport. The notion of a nation was beyond their imagination. Of the 36 children, only seven had ever seen the Gulf of Mexico located exactly four miles from the school. Five children had books, second hand ones, in their homes. One child's father had been gassed at Parchman Prison and he was "glad to be rid of him." Roosevelt's favorite sport was watching his older brother "getting booty in the bushes."

The children's favorite food was baloney sandwiches.

One of the boys named Jamal said when he grew up he was "going to knife the bad man what run off with his momma because he don't like staying with his Auntee."

At the end of each day, I was exhausted. My mind simply could not fathom the deprivation the children endured.

In hopes of establishing some rapport, I read stories out loud. As I read one about a grasshopper, the children were noisy and restless as a hive of bees. I put down the storybook and asked why they weren't listening to me.

"Teacher," asked one of the boys, "what's a hopper grass?"

After correcting him, I explained and received blank stares. It dawned on me that these children didn't have grassy yards.

The long stretches of faded row houses and the bleak, colorless schoolyard flashed across my mind. Something simple, like grass, was almost foreign to them. The children lived, breathed, ate, and survived in a world of poverty.

Poverty of knowledge.

Poverty of resources.

Poverty of spirit.

Night and day I searched for solutions. Over time, I became convinced there would not be an ultimate, universal solution. All that could be done — and should be done — is what one person can do in his or her small space.

I could make a difference in this one class, at this one school, in this one town. And my sanity and salvation — literally my sense of purpose — seemed to hinge on it.

I had been unsuccessful in teaching the students to read. I'd tried flash cards, word families, songs, rhythm, and the organic method. Nothing worked.

One morning, when I was preparing for the reading lesson, handing out papers and pencils, I noticed an empty desk.

"Where is Henry Lee?" I asked.

"He in the bathroom," a girl answered.

"Okay," I said, "let's wait for Henry Lee."

I noticed the bathroom door at the back of the room was wide open. I walked toward the room and looked in.

Henry Lee was standing on top of the toilet seat holding tight to a black crayon. He was writing a word on the bathroom wall.

Henry Lee, who could not even write his own name, wrote a word in crayon on the bathroom wall.

I stared in disbelief. Like an electric shock, an idea came to me.

I ran to the front of the class, picked up a piece of chalk, and wrote on the blackboard in huge letters the very word Henry Lee had written on the bathroom wall.

"All right, Class," I asked, "what is this word?"

Snickering, but in unison, the children said, "SHIT!"

"Wonderful! Fabulous!" I screamed over the ruckus of laughter.

I covered the "S" with my hand and asked, "Now, there is another word on the board. Can anyone tell me what it is?"

Silence.

"Take away the snake sound off the word," I hinted, "and what is left?"

Suddenly, Twana said, "Hit!"

I swept Twana up in my arms and twirled her around. "That's right! You are correct!" I put her down, went back to the blackboard and wrote "HIT" beside the first word.

"Now, Class, there is one more word hidden in the word "HIT."

As I covered the "H" with my hand, there was silence.

Then timidly, Inrenie asked, "Is it 'IT'?"

"Yes! Yes!" I squealed. I rushed over to hug her.

Beside the other two words I wrote "IT" in large letters. Boldly written across the blackboard was a basic three-word sentence.

Excitedly, I pointed to the board and said, "Now children, please read this sentence."

Some were standing in their seats, others were clapping their hands enthusiastically, jumping up and down.

In unison, the children screamed, "SHIT HIT IT!"

I breathed a sigh of wonder saying again and again, "You can read! You can read!"

I rearranged the words on the board to read, "It hit shit" and then "Hit it, shit." They could read the sentence regardless of the word sequence.

The next day, I taught them to read and write another series of words: duck, luck and truck.

It was a beginning.

*Family portrait 1972 (L to R, front row) Jane, Jamie, Liz, and Harry
Back row, Neil Jr. and Neil III*

20

Right after Jamie's second birthday, Neil said he was moving out.

I begged him not to leave, to hang in a little longer. I believed tomorrow would be better. I simply prolonged an agonizing situation for all of us.

Two days after Christmas of 1972, Neil said "I need to leave you."

I physically barred the door. I pleaded for him to stay.

Exhausted, with a deep sense of relief and fright, I finally stopped. He moved out.

I didn't know whom I could rely on or whom could I trust.

In my soul I heard God say, *Me. You can only rely on me.* But I didn't have a strong enough faith.

Bachelorhood seemed comfortable for Neil. I didn't have a comfort zone.

Neil had rented an apartment and was eager to furnish it. He asked when he could come collect his things.

I did not think I could bear to have our children watch him remove his favorite things from our home. I wasn't sure they would understand... neither would I.

To avoid that unpleasantness, I planned a spontaneous trip to Disney World. I thought an escape, a fun time, might be just what my children needed.

I called Harriet, explained the situation to her, and asked if she would keep Jamie. He was too little to make the trip. Then I called Old Dog to see if I could borrow his station wagon. He agreed.

Spur of the moment, I called my friend June Weeks who was also going through a divorce. She had a son, Roland, my Neil's age, and a daughter Lisa, two years older. I invited them to join us on our Disney experience.

"Yes," June answered, without hesitation.

The next morning we piled children, suitcases, games, and ourselves in the station wagon and headed toward Orlando. Just outside of town, a car pulled out in front of us. I blew the horn. The car horn played France's anthem *La Marseilles*. This thrilled the children. We blew again and again, whether needed or not.

To further entertain the young ones, we taught them Pig-Latin. Neil became *Eel-nay*, Roland was *Oland-ray*, and *Lisa Isa-lay*. Harry was too young to play so he just talked, and talked, and talked.

When the older children had mastered Pig-Latin we taught them the I-B language, where you put an I and a B sound after the first syllable of each word. I became *Ji-bane*, June was *Ji-bune*, and Lisa was *Li-bisa*. We were headed to *Di-Bisney Wi-borld*.

None of us could wait to reach Orlando.

At the hotel on the Disney World grounds, Lisa opted to remain in the room instead of having to be with all of us out in the park. She had had enough of my verbose children and wanted some alone time. Neil and Roland took off on their own, leaving June and me to accompany Harry and Liz on the "It's a Small World" ride. After three days of almost continual riding through the canals listening to the song "It's a Small, Small World" I never wanted to hear that music again.

On New Year's Eve we started home again. Halfway there we stopped at a Holiday Inn to rest and to have dinner. Our only request was that June and I have a table to ourselves. Neil and Roland had a table together. Lisa started out at the table with Harry and Liz. After a few minutes, she asked her mother if she could order room service. Harry and Liz dined alone.

The children and I arrived back at our house in Gulfport on New Year's Day, 1973. Neil was gone.

21

I decided to take a cruise with three of my best friends — June, Tish, and Joyce — the spring after Neil moved out. Our soon-to-be ex-husbands agreed to pay for the Caribbean cruise.

Compared to others, we were fortunate. None of us were destitute and we all exhibited an enthusiasm for living in the moment. Most people found it endearing; others not.

We had a bond. Each of us was reeling from rejection, feeling disposed of by our husbands (our length of marriages ranged from 13-18 years). Each of us hoped an ardent lover or the adoration of another man might provide our healing.

On the airplane flying to Florida to board the cruise ship there was an underlying desperation beneath our enthusiasm. If we stopped laughing, tears might start.

We sang on the plane and talked to fellow travelers. I told my three traveling companions that an elderly friend would pick us up at the Miami airport and drive us to the harbor in Ft. Lauderdale where the cruise ship was docked.

Likewise, I told my friend Nathan I was traveling with three elderly female friends.

When I called Nathan — a lifelong friend of mine and Neil's — about meeting us, he was shocked to hear about my divorce. He has always thought of me as Mama Jane — a straight-laced, forever-married woman.

At the airport, I walked ahead of my three friends and straight into the arms of thirty-five year old Nathan. He was bronzed from the Florida sun, full of vitality, smart and appealing.

"Where are your friends?" Nathan asked, looking around for elderly women.

I pointed over to the three striking, elegant females standing silently, their mouths agape too, ten feet away.

With one look in their direction I burst into laughter.

"Hell," Nathan said, "I've been looking around for wheelchairs."

Never had two sets of people been so delightedly surprised with each other.

Nathan piled our luggage in the back of a rented station wagon and drove us up the beach to Ft. Lauderdale. The Atlantic was turquoise, the sand a bright white.

Nathan took us to an open-air restaurant on the canal for shrimp, oysters, and crabs. My friends were intrigued by Nathan, as he was with them. They could hardly keep their friendly hands off one another. Joyce sat quietly, her artist's eye taking in his every move.

Several times that day Nathan and I had opportunity to talk. He asked about Neil and the divorce. I confided in him about the nights I stood blocking the front door begging Neil not to leave. I spoke of my last night with Neil and realized I would never again beg him or anyone to stay with me. I was willing to let him go.

To Nathan I confessed to being afraid and relieved at the same time. Afraid of the future and of being alone; of raising four children; of spending a thousand nights without love, without certainty; yet experiencing relief that I didn't have to call bars at night; that I didn't have to live with the fear that he might hurt himself or someone else while driving after drinking; that he might find happiness without me in his life.

Nathan was a compassionate listener.

Mid-afternoon Nathan drove us to the pier where the cruise ship

Tish, me, June, and Joyce on the cruise

awaited our arrival. He saw us through the admission procedure and helped cart our luggage to our stateroom. A realization seeped in slowly, but there it was. I was attracted to Nathan, and he to me, made sweeter because it was unexpected. Sometime between 10:00 am and this moment, I stopped thinking about divorce, children, and future.

I felt tingly, present, and alive.

My friends sensed Nathan and I wanted a few minutes alone. Repeated hugs, powerful suggestions, and outright playful offerings of bodies and limbs were expressed. Then they left us alone. The ship's whistle blew signaling the time for all visitors to leave. Nathan and I stood at the door to the stateroom. He took my hand in his. Our eyes met. His lips touched mine softly, more like breath than flesh. He opened the door and walked out. Almost as if he did not want to, he paused, then turned around to face me. We shared only a look.

With a whispered goodbye, he departed the ship and left me to a week on an Italian cruise line.

My friends and I shared a deluxe stateroom. We dined and danced. We laughed and shared secrets. The four of us drew the attention and pursuit of many of the ship's officers. We were busy having fun. As we dined on rich food, others were having their cocktails. Since none of us consumed alcohol, we invented our own drink, a frosted, fruited ficken. The name was a conversation piece as we flirted with the bartenders and waiters. The sensuous ambience was the perfect setting for saying goodbye to our previous lives as we anticipated what the future might bring.

Roses, uncorked champagne, and gifts were delivered to each of us from Italian speaking suitors, as were messages of love and desire, a few hidden in empty matchboxes.

Joyce's comment the first night at dinner was, "The Lord said, 'Let there be horniness', and then He created Italy!" That proved to be truer than any of us anticipated.

Perhaps it was my newly acquired trauma-induced leanness, or my wounded spirit which I wore like an aphrodisiac that attracted the captain. But attracted he was. The first night aboard ship with the full moon's reflection dancing on the choppy waves, he escorted me for an after dinner walk, declared his undying love for me and urged me to alleviate his irresistible urge to "maka love." I was not interested in his romantic declarations, but I did not understand this lack of response only served as a challenge to the Italian captain – a challenge he felt must not remain unconquered. The battle was on.

When he returned to the Captain's deck, I raced back to the room to share my experience with the others only to discover that my three friends were also on the quarter deck being similarly propositioned by the First Mate and his staff.

The next day we explored the ship. Somehow, we found everything hilarious. The Chinese valet's name was "Theng Fook Yu." The two elderly Jewish women from New York in the room next to ours tried to hide the fact that the two gay gigolos were their live-in escorts. The floral arrangement sent by friends from home was complete with balloons which turned out to be helium filled condoms.

We each danced with a black man, Mel, the featured entertainer on board who made guest appearances on *All in the Family*. Mel was intrigued by his new southern friends and called each of us "Mizz Scarlet."

I watched two men dance the tango together and thought it was beautiful. I realized what it meant to be 34 and single. I could make decisions on my own without regard to Neil's thoughts or feelings. Two attractive men pursued me. The Captain vied for my attention; so did Edward, the casino operator.

The captain called Edward "thata no good slot machinist."

Our first excursion was Port-Au-Prince. The Captain and First Mate escorted the four of us to Le Claire, Le Habitacion, a resort secluded in the mountains of Haiti overlooking the port city. We drove from the docks up to Le Claire through stark poverty. I saw a naked infant crawling in a lean-to made of discarded refrigerator boxes. Scantily clad native men urinated on the street corners. Large baskets of long loaves of bread sitting outside of hole-in-the-wall shops were the only signs of food. There was an abundance of tropical beauty darkened by rampant poverty. I saw this third world country and my problems seemed inconsequential in comparison.

Le Claire, the favorite hideaway of Liz Burton and Richard Taylor, was too lush for my tastes but the Captain loved the splendor and felt certain it would be the scene of my seduction. I disappointed him again.

In a more quiet manner, Edward, the "slota machinist" also attempted to seduce me. I enjoyed his company and the day after we sailed from Haiti to Puerto Rico, he and I walked down the side streets of San Juan's famed waterfront. Edward bought me a pair of primitive fertility wall hangings made from old Pepsi Cola signs.

I returned to the ship, grabbed my glasses and book, and went to the lounge area to relax among the other idle females who were sunning. We were reading when we heard a growling sound.

I looked up. The Captain was standing over me. He wore Bermuda shorts, his button down shirt was open, and he banged his hairy chest with both fists.

"Whatsa matter," he screamed. "You no lika my body?"

I cringed. Twenty books closed and forty eyes looked my way. I said nothing and slid down in my deck chair.

"I senda you flowers," he ranted, " I senda you love notes. I tella you are beautiful, and you refusa to come to my bed. You lika slota machinist better? It's no possible. I no understanda."

I couldn't bear his egotism — or outburst — and I bolted from the deck.

June was in our stateroom when I arrived. I told her about the captain's embarrassing display and she shrieked with laughter.

I found myself joining in.

That night, we decided to go all out for the Captain's Ball. I knew it would only intensify his desire to seduce me, but after the way he embarrassed me, I didn't care.

I borrowed Tish's gown slit dangerously high up both legs and the V at the neck too deep to be decent. I wore it anyway. We piled my hair on top of my head, applied makeup with extra care, sprayed perfume until we nearly choked, then admired our handiwork.

I looked sophisticated and windblown . . . with a touch of harlot thrown in.

When the dinner bell rang, June, Joyce, Tish, and I put on our tallest high heeled shoes and sashayed down the stairs to dine once more with the Captain at his special dinner. The Captain drooled in his *soup du jour* and breathed heavier than normal through the fish and salad. After dinner, he swallowed his pride, and with genuine graciousness invited the four of us to tour the Captain's quarters. Enrico, the First Mate, accompanied us. Against my better judgment, but enjoying the occasion and feeling there was safety in numbers, I agreed to go. The Captain showed us his personal library and I was impressed with the quality and number of books. He was being a perfect gentleman. We all entered his private living quarters and stepped carefully over the raised threshold. Enrico abruptly whisked the others out the door and slammed it shut. I raced toward the door but the Captain intercepted me and began to reassure me. He told me about his family in Italy, his wife and children, his youth in Naples. It intrigued him I was from Mississippi for he was a William Faulkner fan. He told me that all Italian school children were required to read Faulkner. He gave me a gift, an autographed copy of one of Faulkner's first novels, *Mosquitos*, which was written in New Orleans. It was inscribed — not by William Faulkner — "With a love and desire forever, Captain Iago Lumbrusto".

Captain Iago Lumbrusto and his first mate

We sat on the couch in his spacious living area and acted civilly toward one another. He asked me if it was my religion that prevented me from making love to him. When I nodded and said, "Southern Baptists traditionally do not fornicate." He told me what a good acolyte he had been in Naples and what a good mass goer he was.

He gently took my hand, kissed it, and said, "What possible harm could come from kissing your arms, eyes, breastsa…"

I jerked away from him.

I still believed nice southern ladies did not make trouble by aggressive acts of self-defense. So I sat there like a D.D.H

"Listen," he said to me. "I prova to you I'm a good lover. You see I have a beautiful wifa — and I maka healthy bambinos."

With that, he jumped up and said, "Waita minute. I go get a photograph of my wifa and children to show you."

He was attempting to win me over by showing me a picture of his wife and babies?

I needed divine intervention to get me out the door while still maintaining good manners.

I heard drawers sliding open and shut in another room and thought he was having a difficult time locating the photograph. He came back and when I looked up the Captain was completely naked and very much aroused. His enlarged Italian manhood was eye level. And his Captain's hat was still perched at a dignified tilt on his head.

I threw my head back and laughed.

He thought I was laughing at his now slumping manhood, but it was the situation that amused me. I ran to the door, unlocked it, and rushed down three flights of steps skipping every other one. I entered my stateroom hiccupping with laughter. I knew the Captain would from this moment on leave me alone.

I did not feel a measure of remorse.

As our vacation was coming to a close, we came to the realization that real life awaited us and our responsibilities beckoned.

• • •

A few months after we returned, while I was shopping at Sears at the Edgewater Mall during its 10th anniversary celebration, a man and woman with a large camera approached me.

"May we take your photo?"

"Sure," I said, embracing my new sense of freedom.

Then they asked me for my phone number.

The next week, we entered an agreement for me to go with them to Sears stores in New Orleans and Baton Rouge to model their new makeup made especially for blondes and redheads.

They made posters to promote their new product, but they didn't have the budget to print in color. My features were too bland for back and white pictures. They paid my time and travel (and gave me free products) but eventually broke the news that I wasn't compelling enough in black and white. I think their exact words were "Your features are too bland for black and white."

We parted ways.

I had enjoyed the work, so June and I started modeling for Shamis' Dress Shop in Gulfport.

While modeling, June and I spent weeks thinking about fun ways to occupy our time that would also produce income. Then we had an idea.

We drove to Washington, D.C. to seek information from the Small Business Administration about the sustainability of a ladies dress shop in south Mississippi. The SBA agent spent three days discouraging us. He gave us data indicating ladies dress shops failed more often than any other business endeavor. We were not discouraged.

June and I opened a dress shop named "As You Like It." Our motto was the Shakespearean *"May fair thoughts and happy hours attend you."*

Modeling for Shamis' with June

We enjoyed learning a new business, decorating the shop, and planning trips to seasonal markets. We worked hard in the daylight hours and played hard at night. Escape was our destination. We never judged or criticized, only supported one another.

We spent weekend nights dancing with friends like the Monk of the Month, a delightful seminarian whom we nicknamed Monkey, and his friend, the Alaskan Flash. The Flash had been pumping oil in Alaska too long and his dance technique mimicked his work. He pumped my arm up and down rapidly and jerked back and forth in a frenzy, taking me with him most of the time. It was like dancing with a jackhammer dressed in a leisure suit. I wondered how I was going to explain a whiplash injury to my children who were spending time with their father while I was distracting myself from my motherly duties.

In keeping with our need to escape, we flew to Merida to purchase native garments and silver jewelry for our shop. Merida was a city of pastels and open-aired homes. Its streets were cluttered, the parks littered, and colorfully dressed Indians milled about. The city smelled of rotten oranges. We were undaunted and awoke early our first morning to go to the market square. It was swarming with small brown people dressed in bright blues, reds, and yellows. Men were carrying roosters and chickens haphazardly through town. Women toted massive woven baskets atop their heads. The market square echoed with a cacophony of strange voices and sounds.

We realized immediately we were the tallest people in all of Central America. Men gazed curiously up at us and children pointed at us and shouted "Amazona! Amazona!"

In the morning, we toured the city by foot. I never quite got accustomed to the poverty or the noon siestas taken wherever anyone might be — doorsteps, park bench, or street corner.

The houses were built inches from the sidewalks, if there was a sidewalk, or right on the curbs of streets. The homes were open with iron-grilled work for doors and windows. I saw no screens or glass. It was like being in a stranger's living room.

As our buying trip came to an end, we left Merida with straw baskets filled with native goods and jewelry for our shop.

22

In the year it took to get our dress shop open, I was asked to help with a program for school dropouts. Judge Semski, the Harrison County Youth Court Judge, needed a classroom where troubled youth could continue their studies. My friend Barbara Thompson was already working on developing the school. She asked if I would be the teacher at the newly formed school. In 1973, I taught in Gulfport's first school for dropouts. The students were all wards of the youth court.

There were 35 students in the first class. They had been arrested for such crimes as theft, assault, drug use, and attempted murder. These boys and girls — children in age, ancient in street knowledge — were my constant companions.

As in any group, a leader emerged. A young man named Dennie Ray.

Dennie Ray's effervescent personality and smile made him a likable young man. The other students were drawn to him and followed him willingly. They trusted Dennie Ray. At first they didn't feel the same way about me.

Their world was a place where "every man for himself" reigned supreme. If someone expressed care and concern for them, it was interpreted as manipulation. When I provided special treats for them, it was seen as some sort of bribe to make them do something they did not want to do.

Love and compassion were alien concepts to most of them.

The youth court provided a special Christmas lunch the day before we left for the holidays. As usual, during the lunch break the boys from the class went out to the van to collect the food. We set up a makeshift cafeteria in the wide hallway of the school.

On this particular day, the cooks sent over a large chocolate sheet cake with shiny icing.

Twelve year old Eddie, carrying the tray, could not resist a quick sample. He pinched off a large corner of cake and shoved it quickly into his mouth. Jimmy, a hearty eater, caught him in the act.

The easiest way to make Jimmy's white face red was for someone to be served before him. He derived great pleasure from being first in the lunch line. When he saw Eddie sneak a taste of cake, Jimmy went into a rage. He bolted toward Eddie, put both hands under the tray and shoved the entire cake into Eddie's frail, black face and chest.

With that single act of aggression the War of 11:45 was declared.

The bigger boys came to Eddie's defense. To balance the fight, the girls took Jimmy's side. A full-scale brawl erupted in the hallway. Chocolate cake was smeared, thrown, shoved, stepped on, and ground into eyes, noses, ears, shirts, blouses, and jeans. It was splattered on walls, rubbed on Afros, as well as long blonde hair. The food delivery crew witnessed the havoc, dropped the other food containers on the floor, and buzzed off in the court's van.

I begged, pleaded, yelled, and commanded the students to stop. The students ignored my verbal pleas. One threw a handful of cake in my direction.

I gave up and crouched behind an overturned table.

As I observed this "Chocolate Battle" I began to have an inspiration for the day's English lesson. Perhaps I could use this messy brawl to teach about verbs. Yes, each student writing what he or she had done with and to the cake would be a wonderful way for them to learn about action verbs!

Thinking expansively, I thought that by describing the extraordinary mess, they might learn descriptive adjectives too. Terrific!

Maybe a paragraph, or even a sentence or two strung together with dangling participles might be possible.

They could put down on paper words which expressed their feelings, thinking, and doing. Wow!

Maybe we could even debate the ethics of participating in the War of 11:45.

Better still, a theme written on other wars. A research paper!

Oh, God, I was getting carried away again. Well, maybe for today we would settle for learning action verbs and descriptive adjectives and maybe the correct spelling for a few expletives. I reasoned that if these dropouts had enough creativity and energy to paint graffiti on our school walls, they could spend another few minutes learning to correctly spell "mutherfooker."

The War of 11:45 officially ended at 12:05. One by one the students quieted down. I stood from behind my barricade, brushed a blob of icing off my arm, and glared at the students.

Then I said, "Let's bow our heads for the noon blessing."

"Lord," I prayed, "thank you for this day and for the opportunity of sharing this special dessert. Forgive us for being slobs about it. Thank you for these chocolate covered students. I pray their sugar coating will make them sweeter for the remainder of the day. Amen."

A few shouted "Amen!" Others raced to the bathrooms to wash off their chocolate coatings. Jimmy ran over to the dinner containers, which had been dropped on the floor, and began to serve himself, first.

It was business as usual.

During the four months we'd been together, I realized these teens needed to learn to trust again, to develop a sense of belonging, and of course, to regain some sense of self-esteem and self-worth. Of the 35 students, most had been the victims of physical, emotional, or sexual abuse and neglect.

They had never been shown how to care for others. Or they had forgotten.

After lunch, Dennie Ray, the self-proclaimed leader, called the group to order.

"Ok, listen up. I'm about to speak."

Dennie Ray politely asked me to come to the front of the room.

"Hey, dudes, keep it cool now. We got something special for Teacher."

He turned to me and grinned his most captivating smile.

"Teacher, you been teaching us that giving is better than getting shit. You been trying to teach us caring about somebody else be important to show. Well, most of us disagrees with you. But we thought, 'cause it be Christmas and shit, that we might be willing to try this giving shit. So, from all of us to you, here be a Christmas present."

He handed me a small gift wrapped in newspaper, tied with a large red bow. I read aloud the hand-printed card:

Teacher, you be fine, your face shine
When you looks at us.
Love and kisses from your students

I opened the gift with suspicion. It was a matching gold pen and pencil in a heavy velvet box. As I examined the gift, the unwelcome thought that it might be stolen entered my mind... Maybe one of the boys had heisted the pen set from a local store. I was so sure my suspicion was correct that I was reluctant to accept the gift. Silently, I debated. Should I accept the gift and condone thievery, or refuse it and reject their initial effort in giving to another? I pondered a moment, then accepted the gift, praising them for their care and thoughtfulness.

Most of the students seemed pleased with themselves. As they started leaving for the day, I asked Dennie Ray to remain for a moment to chat with me.

"Dennie Ray," I said, "I appreciate the thought behind this gift. It was a caring and generous thing for all of you to do for me.. I wonder if the pen set might be stolen. If so I would like to find the jewelry store it came from and pay for it. No one needs to know except you and me."

"Teacher," Dennie Ray said, "I don't believe I hearing this! I ain't stole this gift from nowhere. I pay cash money for the thing." He paused for a minute and looked at me indignantly. "I can't believe you think I done stole your present."

"If you didn't steal it, where did you get the cash to pay for it?" I asked.

"Well, see, it's like this. A couple of us dudes pitched in to handle the finances. We pooled our cash. Yeah, we did, Teacher."

"Dennie Ray," I insisted, "where did y'all get this cash?"

He pondered before he answered. With his chin all but touching his chest, he sheepishly responded, "Well, Teacher, me, Jerkhead, and Corky slip off one afternoon, rip off a few cigarette machines, and we had all the cash we needs. You see, I told you once and for all we ain't steal no present. We pay cash money for it 'cause we knows you wouldn't take no stolen present." Then he added, "We don' show it much, Teacher, but most of us dudes loves you."

I still use the pen and pencil set.

TWO & THREE

23

In 1974, I started dating John, a Ph.D. candidate in psychology who had recently left his job as director of music at a Methodist church in Jackson.

He had broken his leg and was on crutches. He took a pain killer while watching television at my home and fell asleep on my living room couch. I covered him up and decided to let him sleep. I checked on my four sleeping children, went to my room, put on my gown, and climbed in bed.

I woke up to a thudding sound and a shrill cry. I jumped out of bed, turned on the lights, and ran outdoors toward the screams.

John was on the gravel drive, his crutches scattered. A huge man in dark clothing and a stocking cap pulled down over his face was slamming his fists into John's sides. Thinking only of John, I ran over to the two fighting men and tried to pull the attacker off of John. He didn't budge. I screamed for him to get off to no avail. In the struggle, the man's shirt rode up his torso. I took one look at the exposed flesh and bit into it as hard as I could. He swung and connected with my face. I fell back on the ground, stunned.

A wailing siren pierced the night air. The man jumped up and threw his stocking cap in the bushes. I recognized the man was a neighbor, Lewis. He was a law enforcement officer and his wife was a friend of John's.

A police car pulled up in front of my house. I crawled over to help John up. He was hurt. I glanced over and saw Lewis pull out his badge as he talked to the policeman in the car.

To my dismay, the police car left. I yelled for it to come back.

Lewis told me to shut up as he pocketed his badge.

I helped get John to the porch. He sat on the steps and I started into the house to get a cool rag for him. Lewis ordered me to stay put.

He held a large flashlight with tape wrapped around the handle. He held it with one hand and repeatedly slapped it into the open palm of the other. Without warning, he slammed the flashlight into John's face with such force that John fell back onto the concrete porch, out cold.

I was frozen, paralyzed with fear for John, for me, for my children.

I needed to get to a telephone. Lewis would not allow me to touch John or tend to him. We sat there and slowly John regained consciousness and managed to sit up.

We listened as Lewis ranted about his wife and John and their varied acts of infidelity. At 3:00 a.m. Lewis left. John drove himself to the hospital. He had three broken ribs and facial lacerations. I called the police. I was told that Officer Lewis Dews had been to my house to investigate a domestic problem. According to the officer on the phone, a law enforcement officer was already at the scene. Two men had fought at midnight in my yard, he explained, over another woman. The entire episode had been documented as a domestic problem between John and me.

Outraged, the next day I called three different lawyers, explained the circumstances, and was told by all three to forget it.

That afternoon, Lewis' attorney called me and asked me to come to his office. He told me that John's life was in danger, but he would do all he could to prevent John's early demise. By the next day John had been fired from his job.

Later that same day, Lewis walked by my house. I was outside with my children. He apologized for getting me involved, but said through clenched teeth, "I'm going to get that preacher boy of yours so he better get out of town."

I did not know where to turn for help. Perhaps it was best to forgive and forget. I tried.

Lewis stalked John — and me — constantly. He even taped telephone conversations between John and me and recounted them to us when he happened to run into us.

Out of desperation, I called my Aunt Vi, a lawyer, for help. Vi and I, without John, met with Lewis and his attorney. Lewis denied everything. He was supported in this deception by his attorney.

Aunt Vi, who was a clerk for U.S. District Court Judge Dan Russell, went into full-assault attorney mode. She told them that if anything happened to me (as an aside, she said she didn't really care about John) each one of them would answer to her.

Reprimanded, Lewis and his attorney remained seated and silent.

Despite Vi's admonishment, Lewis' harassment continued for months. Unmarked cars tried to run John off the road. Lewis frequently made late night phone calls to my home assuring me that he knew every move I made. Lewis told me I could be found any time night or day.

"All I have to do is get on my radio and say the words, *Where is Baby Jane?*"

Then, he explained, lawmen across the Coast would call him back to tell him where I was . . . and who I was with.

Each avenue I explored for relief was a dead end. I felt violated, invaded, dehumanized. When friends came to my defense, they were threatened. Two friends who attempted to gain proof of police neglect were jumped and badly beaten. They were warned to stay out of it. One by one my friends stopped trying to help, and I quit asking. I could not jeopardize anyone else. The harassment became a part of my daily life.

For four months, John looked for other jobs. Finally, he was offered one at a state university. Unbeknownst to me, when questioned about why he hadn't worked in four months, he told the hiring committee about the harassment. He excused it away as my problem, not his.

When John accepted the job, he asked me to marry him.

I said *yes*.

I'd always wanted to live in a college town.

June, me, and Marcia Taylor at my second wedding

24

John and I married in Gulfport in 1975. After the ceremony we went home to hug my children and get our bags.

The phone rang. It was Lewis.

"We're going to have fun in Florida on our honeymoon," he said.

Depressed and tired, we decided to skip our honeymoon and drive straight to Starkville. I spent a week looking for an apartment, making arrangements to move, and returned home to collect my children and furniture.

Neil was about to start his ninth grade year at Bayou View Junior High. He was president-elect of the student council. He was also the quarterback of the football team. He wanted to stay in Gulfport and live with his father (who was still drinking). I couldn't bear to leave Neil, but he was adamant. I rationalized that my daddy lived just a few doors down and would be available if needed. My sister Harriet taught physical education at Neil's school and she willingly agreed to serve as his surrogate mother.

I suffered over the situation. How could I leave my son? I spent night after night in deep prayer. I felt agonizing guilt. Yet deep down, I knew it was the right thing to do. I agreed to Neil's request.

As the moving van pulled away and I put Harry, Liz, and Jamie in the car with me, I turned to look at my first born, standing alone. I cried. I could not help thinking I sacrificed Neil on the altar of my own need to begin life anew. I was once again reminded the right thing is not always the safe thing.

• • •

University life was all I had hoped it would be. I liked our new neighborhood and I loved John's two female bosses — Dr. Marilyn Purdy and Dr. Gail Cotton. I became friends with them both.

In spite of all the hardship during our courting months, I wanted our marriage to work. I wanted a family for my children and a good role model for my boys.

With this second marriage, I inherited two boys. One, smart and adaptable; the other, a challenge. These two stepsons, deemed perfect in every way by their father, were blended with my three sons and one daughter.

John saw my children as out of control and in need of "fixing."

To handle this mix of the perfect and the flawed, I needed skills. Skills I did not possess, like negotiation skills or telling John to drop dead.

Better judgment prevailed and I tried to be an adequate stepmother. The word "stepmother" is an appropriate title. Most of us would like to step out and away from the step-family situation.

It is easier, but not necessarily more rewarding, for us to love and accept a child of our womb than one who appears in our living space via someone else's invitation. I struggled in the role of stepmother in a blended family.

My daughter Liz, the token girl in our family, gave a candid view of her stepfamily in this section of an autobiography she wrote as a school assignment in the fifth grade.

"My mom, who is my real mom, is the greatest mom in the whole wide world, even though my Sunday School teacher says it's not nice for someone to be married two times.

But my mama is nice anyway, and I'm lucky to have a real daddy and a stepmother who's real, real young, and a step-daddy, and they're all nice too, even though they've all been married two times, except my stepmom who has only been married once — but she's young and there's still time for her to make it two. My step-daddy is real nice, too, some of the time. He takes me bike riding on the hills, but the last time we went, I had a crash and broke my bike and he said he would buy me a new one, but he never did. He bought himself one though.

My five brothers are nice some of the time, too, but only three are real and two are step, but my stepfather says to forget the "step" and make them real. And they are nice too, well, except when they are mean and when they get their own way and I never get mine, but my mom doesn't yell at them any more or any louder than she does at me."

I called a conference with her teacher for 8:00 am the next morning and took special care to dress conservatively!

Early in my marriage to John, it became clear that most of the responsibility for all things to run smoothly in our blended family fell directly in my lap. I was responsible for the safety, nourishment, and development of two children whose birth mother threatened to file lawsuits against us in custody matters. I nicknamed her *Sue*.

I hesitated to discipline or even make suggestions to either one of her children for fear of being arrested for child abuse.

The night my step-teenager had his first date in my bank-owned car, he failed to come home by the agreed upon time of 11:00 pm.

When he was not home by 11:30, my overactive imagination envisioned him dead on a dark road, the car smashed against a bridge abutment, or his body lying separated from his head near train tracks.

By midnight I visualized his bloody shirt and wondered how I would explain that to Sue, who was meticulous about having her sons arrive for monthly visits in starched, spotlessly cleaned shirts (in our household, starched anything was a visionary concept).

By 12:30 I had no fingernails left to chew and wondered if I should call the police. Instead I went to the fridge and shoved into my already knotted stomach the leftover lasagna, chocolate pudding, cold peas, and slightly molded Monterey Jack cheese.

I began to plan his funeral.

At 1:15 am, to my immense relief, he casually strolled in, handed me the keys and said, "Hi, Jane. Why are you up so late?"

Soft pedaling my response for fear of Sue, I told him his irresponsible behavior was absolutely not acceptable; it wreaked havoc with my diet and caused cellulite on my already overstocked thighs!

In the morning we talked about it. I explained my fears, and he expressed his need for independence. He tried to allay my fears and I tried to instill in him a healthy fear of the dangers lurking in our world. Like most teens, Todd was certain he was invincible. I found comfort in the fact that we were able to have an open, honest, and calm conversation even though nothing was resolved. But by sharing our true feelings we were getting to know and understand each other.

I gathered my family together and we decided jointly on specific tasks and responsibilities. It was important for each one of us to be a part of a team effort, even Dad! Being the only girl, Liz pulled laundry duty. It wasn't long before it was clear it was not fair for a ten-year old girl to do laundry for 8 people every time chores were assigned. From then on, every member of our family did his or her own laundry. Many mothers possess the title of "good mother" simply because they spend large segments of their leisure and working time doing for their children; doing laundry for their children, cooking for the family, cleaning the house for her loved ones.

I refused to lay my good mother image on the altar of *doing* for my children. I consider myself a good mother most of the time, and years passed without my touching a laundry basket other than my own. Initially, it was difficult. After the first few weeks of confusion over amounts of soap to use, when to bleach, shrunken sweaters, and pink tighty whities, the children began to suffer the strangest side effects. They felt a sense of pride in doing something for themselves. They felt needed and important because they were helping me. They felt part of a team effort.

Their self-images grew by leaps and bounds. They learned time management and the importance of being independent. A truly good mother works herself out of a job, I reminded myself. Hidden among the piles of dirty socks and clothes lurking in the corners of closets were important lessons my children needed to learn.

I took my job as mother seriously. It was important to me to raise enlightened, respectful, productive members of society. I tried to help the children become aware of and respect individual differences within the family, while at the same time I wondered how my own children could be so different from one another.

Neil and Harry were raised identically. They were disciplined, encouraged, held, praised, played with, and scolded the same.

On Harry, the training took hold, while Neil remained unscathed and untouched by reason.

Harry had responsible friends. He did well in school. He succeeded in music. He worked nights as a dishwasher. He paid his own way. He was obedient, mopped floors, and cleaned his own room. He even did windows!

Neil had friends who liked to sneak into The Dream Room strip club in Biloxi. At home, he left a trail of wet towels between the back bathroom and his front bedroom. Every piece of furniture, antique or polychrome, was his personal clothes rack. He never mopped, cleaned, washed, or studied. But he was gifted in the art of stacking, propping, hiding clothes, and sleeping. He got by on his good looks, charm, and sense of humor . . . rarely being held accountable for his actions and procrastinating on chores until someone else finally performed them on his behalf.

How were my sons so different?

Through the mandates of my husband who was studying to be a counselor, we had family councils in which we tried honesty with one another. Usually the sessions ended in screaming affairs where blame bounced around as if we were on a volleyball court instead of gathered around the dining room table.

Neil, III, who lived with his father, but spent the summers with me, was forced by John to attend these sessions. Neil showed his contempt by sucking and chewing through entire sleeves of Halls cough drops, which he preferred to candy.

He threw the individual, tiny paper wrappers behind the only comfortable couch we owned. This was the couch on which he reclined for hours and hours in lieu of doing his chores, claiming he needed to rest to keep his brain sharp for the debate team and to plan for his future.

Months later, after he'd returned to Gulfport, I moved the couch to vacuum behind it. There were hundreds of dust-covered cough drop wrappers. Had he been in the house I'd have . . . well, let's just say "held him accountable."

The stepbrothers, Todd and Harry, also couldn't have been more different. Todd was 17; Harry was 16. Todd was diligent, quiet, short-tempered, and liked rock music played loudly. Harry was spontaneous and cheerful, talked incessantly, was a perfectionist, was stubborn beyond belief, and enjoyed classical music played softly. The Victorian home we lived in had a large, livable attic space. Putting these two in one room was unthinkable, but we did. We had to.

They managed to get along with each other far better than the rest of us. We left it to them to decide how to cope with one another, the only stipulation being they *would* cope. Their solution was one I never dreamed of. Harry was boss of the room and got his own way on Mondays, Wednesdays and Saturdays. Todd was boss and had his own way on Tuesdays, Thursdays and Sundays. On Fridays, they avoided each other and the room. It worked.

Television was limited in our household. Only one hour per day was permitted. The statistics showed high school graduates had watched

18,000 hours of television as opposed to spending 15,000 hours in the class-room. Where did this leave education? Attention spans? Our children were shock-proof from violence and pornography.

To curtail television viewing, I encouraged conversation. We talked as we played chess, backgammon, and Othello. I have to admit I became weary of being beaten by brainy, cunning kids!

Weather permitting, I sometimes invited one or more of our children to go out at night and lie on the trampoline. Together, lying on our backs, we watched the night sky for satellites and shooting stars. Those moments led to healthy, mind-expanding questions and discussions.

When one of the children was reluctant to talk, I asked questions: "What's up there? How did we get here? What are man and woman that God is mindful of us?"

We talked as we scrubbed floors together, talked as we grocery shopped together, talked as we ate dinner together. If nothing else, I was raising thinkers. I also encouraged the children's sense of humor. I loved to hear them laugh.

Among teenagers, one chin pimple required treatment with $29 ointments; athlete's foot was considered terminal. When Liz wore so much purple eye shadow she looked like Lily Munster, I tried to look at the bright side.

This too shall pass.

It was just part of the maturing process, I told her.

In a crisis we tried to laugh at the situation, not the person. Sometimes it worked.

I tried to let love show. We talked often about the fact that words are cheap. It's action that counts. Love can't just be spoken, it must be shown. I told them, my children of my womb and my children of my marriage to John, constantly and continuously that they were wonderful, they were magnificent, they were fantastic, they were the greatest, they were sensitive, they were caring, and they were loving. It was possible they might never hear those words from anyone else. I wanted to be a good model for the behavior I expected of them, but I failed, often.

As the years passed and the crises became more frequent, I found it easier to solve problems in new ways. At times, I was adept at giving the problem back to the not-so-repentant child who caused it, saying, "I don't have a clue how to solve this. Can you help?"

But sometimes anger and resentment had a way of building up inside of me. I'd never developed a healthy outlet to relieve stress. Stress upon stress upon stress would stack up inside of me until my red headed temper erupted like a volcano. I reverted to childhood. I dealt with unpleasantness with tantrums, slamming doors, throwing dishes, and lamps.

My adult tantrums were more damaging. They had the added awfulness of dangerous, cruel, and ugly words spewing from my mouth. The words were like boomerangs, returning to the sender covered in shame.

At times my children saw these spontaneous and explosive emotions. When Jamie, as an eighth grader, had received his twentieth detention at school, my fury was set loose. When he arrived at home I did not wait for an explanation. As he climbed the steps, I shoved him all the way up, kicking him, screaming at him. I told him if he didn't shape up and behave, I would send him back to Gulfport. I wounded Jamie physically and emotionally. I knew in some way I was the cause of his unhappiness and his sessions in detention, but my rage was uncontrollable.

Neil, Harry, and Liz also experienced the worst of me, usually when they were in need of noble, loving, mothering. Physical violence was rare, but at times it slipped through the chains of my emotional walls.

These episodes taught me I had to learn to control my anger. I could not let the hot lava of ire erupt to damage another. Anger control was accomplished only through a powerful commitment to the truth that my children and loved ones were there for me to protect and love, not to damage.

I don't have many regrets in my life, but those moments are among them.

When I think about what I did to Jamie, I want to find him, hug him, and tell him I'm still so sorry. Jamie's heart is big. He forgave me long before I was able to do the same.

• • •

In the early years in Starkville I worked too much. I had two jobs at the university and attended night school aiming for an Ed. D. During this time another couple joined John and me in opening a restaurant called "Four in the Attic." The menu was geared to college students since the restaurant was located across from campus. Our menu was Po-Boys and Shrimp Gumbo. I added "gumbo cook" to my list of occupations. Every morning at 5 am I cooked gumbo and delivered it to the restaurant, then went to my college job.

Amid the chaos of home life and work, an encounter with my two youngest children enlightened me. I left work early one afternoon and I arrived home early — in time to prepare supper, help with homework, do my own, and put Brent and Jamie to bed. I read them a story, said prayers with them, and demanded they be quiet and go to sleep. I needed a few minutes to myself. Brent and Jamie nodded their consent.

With that affirmation I went to take a shower, color my hair, and relax. As I was massaging in red Clairol, I heard laughing, squealing, and a sound like someone jumping on a bed.

Furious, I climbed out of the shower and wrapped my wet hair in a towel. Soap suds and bright red streaks streamed down my face. I grabbed an old beach towel, threw it around me and stormed into the bedlam.

"Shut up!" I yelled. "Get in the bed! Go to sleep!" I paused for effect. "NOW!"

I turned around and slammed the door.

Then I heard Jamie say to Brent, "Who was that?"

After that, I quit one job and made an effort to spend more time with the children. I even had time for early morning meditations. During a time of reflection, I realized that in this life, only the fittest survive. Animals survive through instinct. Families survive through understanding and tradition. Step families survive through compassion, cooperation, and humor. I applied God's psychology, "Love the Lord your God with all your heart, mind, and soul and your stepchildren as yourself, Amen."

• • •

As we learned to live together as a blended family in Starkville, Lewis, the ATF agent from the coast, continued to harass John and me.

John took down the license tag numbers of cars, many with darkly tinted windows,that attempted to run him off the road. Our second summer in Starkville, we took Liz and Todd to California for John to attend a course at Andrus Gerontology Center.

We stayed with Wendy and Ken, cousins from the White side of the family. On the way to California we camped in the red wood forests and other campsites. We felt free from being watched and threatened

When we returned to Starkville, I received a phone call.

"I had your little girl in the sights of my rifle while you camped out," a man said.

I slammed the phone down. It was 2:00 a.m. but I called Clay Simmons, both a boss and a friend, and told him about the call.

He came over and brought an Assistant District Attorney with him. They heard the story from start to finish. The next morning, a law enforcement officer installed a tape recording device on our phone. They told me: *If he calls again don't hang up. Record the conversation.*

The calls kept coming. I delivered the tapes to the sheriff who, in turn, delivered them to the District Attorney's office. The FBI was called in.

Each telephone call — whether from the anonymous stalker or

from Lewis himself — confirmed that we had been followed all the way to California. They knew where we ate, where we camped, and what hotels we stayed in.

I was terrified it would never end.

A few months after our California trip, I received a call from my good friend Harry Simpkins. Harry lived on the same street as Lewis in Gulfport. Harry was a member of the Coast Crime Commission. He said Lewis had applied for the job as head of that commission.

Harry, in addition to knowing Lewis personally, knew about the year of stalking. He wanted to know if I would be willing to be interviewed by the commission regarding the harassment.

"Absolutely," I said. "The man is a maniac and doesn't need to be anywhere but an asylum!"

Lewis did not get the job.

When he discovered he didn't get the job, he called to threaten me because of the "lies" I told about him. I told him the call was being recorded and the sheriff would receive it immediately.

The calls trailed off.

About a year later, I heard he had a terminal case of cancer.

The calls finally stopped.

• • •

At eight o'clock in the morning, on June 21, 1983, I was at my desk on the 4th floor of the Bost Extension Center on the campus of Mississippi State University. My phone rang. It was Harriet.

"Hi, Jane. You better see if you can come home. Daddy's had a heart attack and isn't doing well."

I panicked.

"He's in intensive care at Memorial Hospital," she said. "They called an ambulance last night about midnight. When we got to the hospital Daddy told me not to call you. But you need to be here."

"Of course! I'll leave right away."

I went to Dr. Marilyn Purdie's office to tell her that I needed to leave. She told me to go immediately and to let her know if she could do anything for me.

I went across the hall to tell John. He told me to leave but to take Harry with me. Neil and Liz were vacationing in Walloon Lake with their father. John said he would take care of Jamie, Todd, and Brent.

Harry and I drove to Gulfport and arrived mid-afternoon. We went to intensive care. The nurse let us in to see Daddy. He was awake and reached for my hand. It felt cold.

He whispered, "I love you."

He saw Harry, his namesake, and tears filled his eyes. "Hey, Boy." He tried to talk, but shook his head.

"I love you, Daddy. Please hang in there." I said. "We need you. Do what the doctor says and maybe you can go home soon."

He tried to smile. "Maybe," he mouthed.

Harry leaned over to hug him. Daddy put his arms around Harry and held him. Both cried. I had to leave; I needed air. On the way out of his room I saw Dr. Nievas, Daddy's physician.

"He is going to be ok, isn't he?"

"It's iffy," he said, "His heart is not healthy. We are doing all we can."

I thanked him.

Harry followed me out and we met Harriet and Rachel, Daddy's wife, in the waiting room. The four of us sat together.

Harriet looked over at Harry.

"No matter what happens," she said, "Daddy will want you to go on this weekend to the Lion's Band Camp. Daddy is so proud that you're first chair again."

"I'm not sure," he said. "I need to be in both places."

So like your mother, I thought. *Needing to be in two places at once.*

I realized Harriet and Rachel had been at the hospital since midnight. I told them to leave. Harry and I would stay. They left instructing me to call if there was a change. The afternoon wore on. I called Neil III at Walloon Lake. I told him about his granddaddy.

"We will leave right now," he said. "I'll go by Starkville to pick up Jamie."

Harry and I sat quietly. Every so often Harry would ask about Daddy and his health. Evening arrived. Harry curled up on the couch to doze. I could not sleep. At ten o'clock Harry woke from his nap and said, "I'm going down to the chapel to pray for Granddaddy."

"Ok, pray hard."

He left and I thought how blessed I was to have a sensitive, caring son. I regretted that Neil and Liz had to leave their vacation, for they had just arrived in Michigan two days earlier. I sat in semi-darkness and silently prayed, asking for strength and wisdom. Suddenly there was a great deal of noise. An alarm echoed through the hospital. I looked up and saw Harry running down the hall.

He yelled at me, "Granddaddy is dying. Do something."

He grabbed me and held me sobbing. We stood arms around each other. It seemed like only moments when the doctor came out to say my daddy had died.

I called Harriet first. She called Rachel and they came back to the hospital. We were all tired, but more so, bereft. It was all too sudden. We had no time to prepare.

After Daddy was released to the funeral home. The four of us went to Harriet's house to rest. The next day, as we waited for Neil, Liz, and Jamie, we made funeral arrangements. I called John. He picked up Todd and Brent and came that afternoon. I called my two mentors at State, Dr. Gail Cotton and Dr. Marilyn Purdie. They both came down the next day.

The visitation at the funeral home was packed. Daddy had many friends. My children's father Neil and his wife Jill came. Harriet and I asked Neil Jr. to be a Pall-bearer. He was honored to do it. Since it was Friday, Harriet and I insisted Harry go on to Itawamba to the band camp. Dr. Gail Cotton drove him there.

At the graveside the next day, I was in a contemplative frame of mind. Fleeting memories of Daddy through the years consumed me. I'd always been afraid of displeasing him. I remembered his demands that I be a good girl at all times. I recalled the strictness with which he dealt with me; yet always laced with humor.

But then a thought that had been hidden away for decades began to float to the forefront. Daddy wanted me to be who he needed and wanted me to be. I thought I could not be the real me.

As he was lowered into the ground, and the pallbearers placed roses on the coffin, I could not help but think, "at last I am free."

But that awareness brought with it a burden of guilt I never quite dispelled.

25

John and I worked together at the university. During a week-long workshop on aging, I noticed that an attractive young participant was smitten with my charming husband. I was amused by it because I felt confident and secure in the love he and I shared.

On Friday the workshop ended at noon. John and I had planned to spend the afternoon together relaxing and recovering from the presentations.

I waited at home until nearly two o'clock. When he didn't come home, I became concerned and called his office. His secretary told me he had left at noon to go jogging.

Annoyed that he had forgotten our afternoon plans, I walked over to the jogging track to look for him. I took a short cut across campus, crested a hill behind one of the dormitories, and saw my husband's car parked far below on the edge of the woods that surrounded the campus.

I stood on the grassy field and felt a knot in my stomach.

It was springtime and the woods below were bursting with color—muted whites of dogwood, lavender of red bud trees, and the reds and purples of azaleas. Their colors and fragrances filled that sunny afternoon with a crisp freshness —the opposite of what I was feeling.

I scanned the scene below. I noticed movement behind one of the stately pines. There was my husband sensuously caressing the young, fair-haired lady from the workshop.

I was devastated. Tears filled my eyes. I fell to the ground. I denied what my eyes witnessed. The current source of love and affection, but the bane of my children's existence, was giving himself away to someone else. Unable to stand or move or stop watching, I felt betrayed.

I sat on the damp grass trying to talk sensibly to myself, trying to rationalize his behavior, trying to excuse him.

Finally, I managed to stand and somehow make my way back home.

In the days that followed, I recognized my dependence on John for my sense of well-being. Every time I relived the scene, I became sick with jealousy and shame. I confronted John. As a counselor himself, he attempted with psycho-babble to convince me it wasn't his fault. I allowed his behavior to rob me of my confidence. I lost faith in us.

The pain of rejection, along with humiliation, opened the floodgates. Self-pity filled the void where only days ago joy, love and anticipation reigned.

Hysteria was easy and I gave in to it for a while. Perhaps I would have succumbed totally had it not been for the loving support of my children and friends.

These words echoed silently and continuously in the deep recesses of my memory. "God has not given me a spirit of fear, but one of power, and love, and a sound mind."

The days and weeks that followed were filled with accusations and raw pain. In an attempt to put some order back into our lives I suggested we give ourselves some time and space. My hope was to re-build our relationship on a stronger foundation.

We agreed to a trial separation.

• • •

When I was five years old, Harriet hosted a Halloween party for her friends. She invited only boys and other tomboy girls. No girlie girls or babies allowed. Harriet and her friends played football in the backyard before eating Halloween cookies and pecan pie.

I was not included in the party. It was an injustice — a separation I could not tolerate.

The day was cool and overcast. My beloved Floy wrapped me in my coat and hat and took me by the hand to go for a walk. When I realized I was being pulled away from the party, I grabbed Harriet's skinny leg and would not let go. She kicked and jerked, but I held on tight as my wails and screams grew louder. Mother and Harriet tried again and again to pry me loose.

Harriet's friends chanted, "Cry baby! Cry baby!"

I screamed even louder. I was not going to let that party happen without me.

Floy finally coaxed me off of Harriet with the bribe of a large, round butter cookie with raisin eyes. I took the cookie and reluctantly consented to go for a walk, as long as Floy brought along more cookies.

Hand in hand, Floy and I walked to Bailey Woods crunching crisp, brownish red leaves underfoot. The cool breeze whipped between the trees. I carried my hurt and rage with me.

In the woods, we found a rotting stump to sit on. Slimy, curly mushrooms were growing on the sides of the stump. I touched one. For some reason it made me gag.

I sat on the stump sulking. I swung my legs out and then banged my shoe heels into the stump. Again and again. Thump! Thump! Thump!

I felt empty. My sister — and mother — did not want me. I felt abandoned. It seemed as if my whole world had come to an end.

Floy tried everything to comfort me. She embraced me and tickled me. She sang to me and offered me more cookies. Then in desperation, she began to quote the 23rd Psalm, probably to calm herself more than me. Floy was Psalm oriented. Over and over she quoted the Psalm, emphasizing in a sing song voice the verse, "Yea though I walk through the valley of the shadow of death, I will fear no evil (meaning me I'm sure) for You are with me."

We sat on the stump for what seemed like an hour. With one great last sniff, I wiped my nose on my coat sleeve and asked Floy to take me home.

Mama hugged me when I walked in the door and asked where Floy had taken me.

"In the shadow of death!" I said.

One evening as the New Orleans bound train was coming down the railroad tracks, an elderly, hard of hearing neighbor drove his new 1940's Ford, complete with running boards, across the tracks onto the path of the train.

The impact woke everyone in the neighborhood. Men rushed to the scene.

Stumbling back down the street, one man ran past us screaming, "He's dead! He lost his head!"

Mrs. Stevens, our across the street neighbor, came and sat on our porch. Through tears she reported, "That poor man's head flew through the air and landed on the north side of the tracks. His twisted body is laying crumpled on the south side. Now, bless his soul, Dr. Farnstock is separated for all time by the L & N railroad tracks."

Horrified, yet curious, I wanted to see death in action. Mama did not allow me or Harriet to go see the remains of the wreck. The idea and mystery of death, and separation, grew inside me. Thoughts of that moon-less night, the screeching crash, the wailing sirens, and the twisted pile of metal consumed me. For a while after Dr. Farnstock's death I squirmed around on the warm grass of early afternoons and imagined him now that his head and body were separated by the train tracks. I could not conjure up any image of him beyond the mutilation.

For the remainder of my childhood, the clanging, horns, and vibrations of oncoming trains awakened in me an ominous presence — and the remembrance of death, destruction, and decapitation.

Separation anxiety has been with me all my life.

• • •

John and I separated and I moved my children again. This time to an old Victorian house that no one wanted. The rent was affordable, but we had to work hard to make the house habitable. Then, suddenly and unexpectedly, John filed for divorce.

Once again I was a single woman with four children to support.

I felt abandoned and betrayed.

I felt separate.

26

I completed my graduate work at Mississippi State University and earned, for the second time, a doctoral degree. But it didn't lead to a better job.

The university's excuse for not promoting me was I had committed an unforgivable sin. Earlier I had diligently worked for two and a half years taking distance learning graduate courses from California. I had earned a Ph.D. .

Some of the professors of education at MSU did not deign distance learning as valid. For them, true learning occurred only in a traditional class-room. However, Sandra Price, my major professor, supported me without hesitation.

I chose to repeat the graduate courses and do it "their" way.

During my oral exams, the faculty asked me to state my life's goal.

"My goal in life," I said, "is to eradicate ignorance in Mississippi."

When the faculty ceased laughing, I defended my statement.

"If you have a life goal you can meet," I explained, "you'll eventually have to form another one, on and on. If your goal is something you know you will not achieve in your lifetime, then every step you take, whether large or small, moves you closer toward your goal. Each step gives meaning, satisfaction, and a sense of accomplishment to your life."

It was an extemporaneous answer. One I'm sure the faculty didn't buy.

Still, they awarded me an Ed. D. The same professors who ridiculed me for my "degree by mail" seemed embarrassed that I quickly — and with high grades — completed their prescribed program.

"Well, of course it was easy for you," they had the audacity to tell me, "You had already done it once before."

I sought comfort in my faith. I promised myself and God to be a good Christian and live my life doing the loving thing.

This led me to want to correct my wrongs and atone for them. I attempted to make things right with John and with our children. I felt a deep need for a complete family — one with mother, father, and children under the same roof.

I arranged to meet with John after nearly two years of separation. On a cold February morning, we agreed to try again.

I had already planned Harry's 11th birthday party for February 17, 1978. I figured, why not kill two birds with one stone? The chapel for my third wedding was the Skate Odyssey in Starkville. Our witnesses: The twelve boys invited to Harry's birthday party.

Harry was sad and embarrassed about our re-marriage. I tried to console him. I leaned over and held his face in my hands.

"Honey," I said, "change is a part of life."

We stared at each other solemnly for a few seconds. Then we began guffawing.

I'd used the same words two years earlier when I tried to comfort Harry about my separation from John.

• • •

John and I lived together for two more years. During that time, my friend and mentor, Dr. Gail Cotton, and two other couples pooled our resources. We purchased Blackjack Stables, a horse farm seven miles east of Starkville.

We owned twenty-six horses and stabled another five for students. We rented out the horses to students to ride through the wooded trails. We took turns playing sheriff and chasing after jocks who wanted to run our horses to death. We all had full-time jobs at the university, so we hired Floyd, a disabled horse-whisperer, to be our stable manager.

Floyd was amazing with the animals. He fed, bathed, and trained each horse in spite of the fact that his legs crossed over one other as he walked. Each step caused him pain. But Floyd needed the job and he relished being there to help younger children learn to overcome their fear of riding.

When we bought new horses at auctions, Floyd was the one who did the selecting. One day he bought a Welsh pony named Dammit. All the children wanted to ride that horse so they could freely yell, "Giddy up, Dammit" without getting in trouble.

When Liz was 11, she fell off her horse. Floyd painfully hurried to her and talked her into getting right back up again. He taught her to face and overcome her fear.

Gail moved onto the property in a house that came with the stables. John and I, tired of the constant upkeep of the Victorian behemoth, bought a double wide trailer and moved our family on the property as well.

Gail and I, the two owners who lived closest to the stables, ended up doing the bulk of the work. We would tend the horses, feed them, and muck out the stalls.

Late one day, after we had cleaned about 15 of the stalls, Gail threw down her shovel and screamed, "What is this! Our partners are able-bodied men with male children. You and I — both with Ph.D.'s —are the ones mucking this shit!"

Gail was right. I was delirious. I was working 40 hours a week at the university, taking care of five children, and spending all my free time shoveling shit.

I'd had enough.

Without thinking, I gathered a handful of horse shit and threw it on Gail.

She retaliated.

We slung poo at one another until we were both covered.

When we finally stopped, I thought about the War of 11:45 at the drop out school in Gulfport. At least what the delinquents threw at one another was edible.

Gail and I, now both unhinged and exhausted, fell into maniacal laughter.

Floyd pulled up in his truck, heard the commotion, and limped over to see what was going on. When he realized Dr. Gail Cotton, always proper, was covered in manure, he almost fell to the ground.

About that time, a car full of sorority girls drove up to ride. When they saw the three of us, they decided another day might be a better time to ride.

Harry, a freshman in high school, had a dream to become a drum major for the band. He found a broomstick and practiced throwing it into the air and catching it. He marched up and down the property conducting and leading his own imaginary band.

Because our double wide was confining, we did not want Harry practicing his saxophone inside. He used the barn as his practice room. He found a receptive audience. When the horses heard him playing, they ran up to the fence and listened. I was in awe of the relationship. The horses swayed their heads as Harry serenaded them.

After the horse shit free-for-all in the barn, I encouraged Jamie, Liz, Harry, and Todd to help with the mucking and feeding. Some days they did so willingly and other days, especially rainy or snowy days, more pressing issues such as homework and study claimed their attention.

Raising five hungry children in the summertime got expensive. We decided to grow our own vegetable garden. None of us were gardeners. Of all the things we planted, only yellow squash grew to maturity.

I sautéed squash.

Harry practicing to be a drum major . . . with a broomstick

I boiled squash.

I put raw squash in salads.

I made squash soup.

The day I barbecued squash, the rebellion started.

All the children and my husband refused to pick, clean, slice, or eat squash ever again.

The stables experience thrilled me, but not so much the rest of the family. Town living seemed the more sensible way to live for my husband and children. Wanting to please everyone and make them happy we moved back into town. I found it confining and boring, but I was alone in those thoughts. I longed for green space, for mornings without the sound of automobiles, for a saddled horse to accompany me on a ride, even if only in my dreams.

27

In 1981 I drove down the Natchez Trace from Starkville, Mississippi. I passed dogwoods blooming under tall, jagged pines. Wild purple azaleas and black-eyed-Susans dotted the roadside, intermingled with prickly blackberry vines. Sun bleached, askew barns interrupted the rolling landscape. The late March sky was azure and hypnotic. I was en route to be the keynote speaker at a senior citizen luncheon sponsored by my employer, the Mississippi Cooperative Extension Service. I was proud of my educational accomplishments and looked forward to sharing my knowledge and expertise.

After driving for two and a half hours, I reached the Hunter's Hollow Community. I stopped to ask directions at a filling station.

"Can you tell me how to get to the Apostolic Lighthouse Pentecostal Church?" I asked.

"Take the ruts through the cotton field," the attendant in overalls said, pointing in a northerly direction, "and keep on going 'til the road run out."

As I drove, I felt like I had stepped back in time.

The plowed fields on each side of the rutted road were dark and rich. There was black dirt on the left as far as the horizon. On the right were freshly planted fields of cotton. The only other vehicle in that vastness was a rusting tractor with spoke wheels. The sky was cloudless.

I came upon the church and pulled my car into a weedy beaten-earth parking lot. The church building was an historic site. It had been built about the time of the Civil War.

On the clapboard siding was a faded sign: "Green stamps save money. Jesus saves lives."

As I entered their meeting, there were forty or fifty elderly people sitting in folding chairs, fanning themselves with cardboard fans that advertised a funeral home. The youngest senior citizen appeared to be close to seventy-five. I guessed a few were centenarians. They had dressed for the occasion. The women wore flowery dresses and multicolored hats with flowers, birds, and other ornate trimmings. The men had on suits and ties purchased decades earlier. Or perhaps hand-me-downs.

These were good people, but they were clearly uneducated and too old to go back to school. I thought of the speech I had prepared and wanted to climb back in my car. I wanted to go back to the university. This was going to be a waste of their time – and mine.

Despite my concerns, I stayed. While waiting to speak, I mingled with a few of the men and women. A man in a wheelchair had his crafts on display. He made birdhouses. I made small talk. One conversation about the spring rains, another about gout. Still another about arthritis.

They had prepared a lunch of fried chicken, turnip greens, buttered corn on the cob, black-eyed peas, and iron skillet cornbread. After everyone had finished, Mrs. Maybelle Almarene Hunter-Smith led the group in a songfest. It was a knee slapping, arms waving, Hallelujah time. With each chord played on the upright piano, her hat, heavy with flowers, fell southward over her forehead in time with her bouncing bosom.

Once the singing was finished, it was time for my speech. I stood up, put my notes on the rickety podium, and deeply regretted the words I had written. I had done my best, but I'd also written to impress, if not to dazzle, my audience. I talked about the concepts of pedagogy and curriculum design, auxiliary studies, and problem posing, the Paideia Proposal and organic reading. I explained how each concept might relate to economic development. My audience moved not a muscle. There was no head nodding, no hand-wringing, no Amens! Not even a cough.

As I leaned forward on the podium to make my last comment, it became clear to me how I could involve these senior citizens. I smiled and said, "You have opportunities in your community to be involved not only in educational workshops, but also in economic development. Many of you are entrepreneurs. You grow flowers that others in the community might want to purchase. You bake delicious cakes and cookies that could be sold. Your homegrown tomatoes and corn can be sources of income. Your crafts are things the public buys at flea markets and retail stores. Use your gifts to make your life better. When you do that, you enrich your community and every life in it."

I nodded my head and said, "Thank you for listening and may God bless you."

Not one person clapped. I picked up my notes and moved toward my seat on the front row. An old, stooped giant of a man stood up and shouted in a raspy voice, "Teacher, please don't sit down. You wait a minute."

I stopped and stepped back from the podium. Slowly he shuffled to the front of the room. He came and put his large calloused hand on my shoulder.

As he towered over me he said, "Teacher, years and years ago, I come to school in this church building. I come here every day for two, maybe three months a year until I was about nine years old. Then my granddaddy needed me for a full day work in the fields. Every day, with an ole mule in front of me walking up and down them furrows, I look over here and see children out in the yard playing. I hear the teacher calling them inside for lessons. I used to stop plowing, trying to hear what the teacher saying. I wanted to hear big words like you say today and I wanted to know what the words mean. I'm 94 years old now. I don't know what you mean by what you say, but I weep with joy I heard a lesson today. God-Almighty knows we need people like you to keep on teaching. Please, don't quit. Don't you quit, ever."

He stopped to take a breath, and then he went on, "I was down in my back this morning. I say to myself, 'there ain't no way I can come here to the meeting.' But when they tell me some teacher from State University going to be here talking about education, I know I had to get up and come. I proud I did. I would have passed on to Glory without ever hearing nothing as exciting as what you said today. You gave us your best. That ain't never been done here by a white teacher before. I thank my Holy Jesus you come here today. And I thank you."

The men and women began to clap. They all stood. An ovation for this giant man. When they stopped, I turned to shake his hand and asked his name. "My name's Washington. They call me Pastor Wash."

I left the church and drove down the dirt ruts that led back to the highway. At the intersection, I stopped the car. I felt humbled and humiliated and a little bit sick. Honored to have encountered Pastor Wash and his congregation. Grateful to have stood in a place rich with history and practical learning. Thankful for people willing to listen to a privileged white woman. Blessed that they accepted me. Yet I was appalled at my arrogance. I'd become lost in theory and nomenclature and those capital letters after my name and with my own expertise and knowledge.

Pastor Wash may have been pulled from the classroom at the age of nine, but he knew a lot more about what really mattered than I.

• • •

John had previously been a minister of music in other Methodist churches, so we joined First United Methodist Church in downtown Starkville. We enrolled the children in Sunday school classes, choirs, and teen programs. John and I both sang in the choir. Jamie and Liz's Sunday School classes consisted primarily of coloring pictures of Jesus, which didn't suit me. I wanted them to learn scripture and what the verses meant.

Harry's group of teens seemed to talk about current events rather than spiritual ones, which I found wanting. Our adult class was more a coffee-drinking social hour.

I had asked the children to sit on the front row during the worship hour while John and I sat in the choir loft so I could watch the children during church. To make sure they behaved.

Harry, who worked late nights at a restaurant so he could stay after it closed to practice his saxophone, was sleepy most Sunday morning. One Sunday as the church service began and we sang the anthem, I looked down to check on the children. Harry was sound asleep. He was leaning so far forward, tottering, I feared he would tumble out of the pew. I motioned to Liz to wake Harry up, but she was engrossed in a book (not the Bible).

In the midst of the scripture reading, there was a thud. Harry fell forward and hit the railing. He stood up and stretched like he didn't realize where he was.

He noticed the congregation staring at him. He bowed and sat back down.

After that, I let Harry sleep in some Sundays.

We had friends in the church. The music program for adults and young people was excellent. But I still felt something wasn't complete. I was searching for a religious confirmation of some kind, but I wasn't sure exactly what I was yearning for.

A small Presbyterian church, which initially met in a room at the university, had just built a chapel in the woods. I talked John into trying that smaller church. I thought intimacy might be what I needed.

We moved our letter and joined Trinity Presbyterian Church. I was more comfortable there because the church had huge glass windows that let nature be part of our worship. That lightness and naturalness spoke to me. And the young minister admitted to still struggling with his faith. He told us, "I don't have all the answers."

Harry, Jamie, Liz, Neil, and me in Starkville

We stayed at Trinity until 1983.

My second marriage to John was no more successful than the first. In some way, I believe, we both wanted more than we could give. Even as we recommitted to solving problems together and tried to build our family, I felt removed from John. We both put effort into our togetherness as a couple — and as a combined family — by taking trips, playing, and praying together.

But John's job —and his penchant for counseling attractive, young, single women —became more consuming.

One such counseling session occurred at the Holiday Inn where my boss was dining. She saw John. He climbed through a tall hedge and crawled into room 209.

My boss told me what she'd seen.

My rage was unleashed. His new car was parked in the university staff lot. I went to the store, bought poster paper, tape, and magic-markers. I wrote curse words and accusations — in large blue, red, and orange colors — on poster board. Then, with tape and scissors in hand, I covered his car, like wallpapering a small room, with filthy thoughts and words. Revenge tasted sweet, but only for an hour or two. Then I felt nothing but remorse.

It was clear I needed a change.

I left John, my university job, and gave away my interest in Four in the Attic Restaurant.

I moved to Oxford with Harry, Liz, and Jamie.

Two months after I left Starkville, John married a girl who looked a lot like me. Except she was five inches shorter, fifty pounds lighter, and many years younger.

FOUR

28

I left one university town and moved to another.

Oxford seemed the logical place to move. My uncle Garner and his wife Francis lived in Oxford. Francis taught anthropology and archeology. Son Neil lived there, too. He was in his sixth year at Ole Miss.

I rented a home on Buchanan Avenue close to the square and enrolled the children in school. I had no job but had applied to work at the university.

In the meantime, with the bills John and I owed in Starkville, which John refused to pay, I filed for bankruptcy. It was a humiliating experience. I became even more frugal than ever.

I did, however, manage to keep my favorite horse from Starkville, Jitterbug. Floyd brought him to Oxford for me. I boarded Jitterbug about a mile out of town and rode as often as possible. The hills surrounding Oxford were fun to race up and down. Riding made me forget, at least temporarily, where I found myself — alone, mid-40s, bankrupt, unemployed, thrice divorced, and with three children to support.

Despite my position in life and the lingering personal pain of rejection, I felt an odd sense of adventure. A new beginning. Through the hurt there came a sort of personal resurrection. A healthier, less dependent Jane was being born. I promised myself I would never again allow a man or a situation to be my God. I could live a meaningful life without the constant presence and continuous affirmations of a man.

I had to think for myself, to experiment, to grow, and to believe.

I was beginning to really understand what I'd read about for years. Wanting to be together, rather than needing to be together, makes the truly happy relationships.

But I still desired adult company. The first months in Oxford were lonely. I did not know anyone other than family. Most evenings, I fed the children macaroni and cheese for supper and helped them with their homework.

Craving some adult interaction, I then went three blocks away to the bar at the Holiday Inn. I sat alone at a corner table, had a bowl of popcorn, and a glass of Chardonnay.

Occasionally, if he wasn't too busy, I visited with Clyde, the bartender. Soon people I recognized strolled in.

A football coach or two usually sauntered in full of themselves with the latest news on "the team." I recognized a politician with great power (he was chair of the Appropriations Committee in the Mississippi legislature) who stood just over five feet tall. I had met him through my work at MSU in the Stennis Institute of Government. When he was at the bar, he'd come over to talk to me.

One night after having a bit too much to drink, he sat down at my table. He'd always been nice and supportive. With a bit of a slur, he asked me to marry him. I thanked him for the kind offer, gently refused, and reminded him that he had a wife at home.

At Halloween, my uncle Garner invited me to go to a party with him. I accepted.

It was a noisy crowd. Garner was busy entertaining the older ladies. That's what Garner did best. Eudora Welty had nicknamed Garner "Dixie-Belle" when they had worked together on a book about Mississippi that was funded through a WPA project. Garner was a dancer, a flirt, and a true southern gentlemen who enjoyed societal conversation, but only with women. Some of the older Oxonians still called Garner Dixie-Belle.

I wandered out to a balcony. I watched people coming and going. I sensed a presence and looked up to see a tall man standing next to me. He spoke with a pronounced New Orleans accent.

He asked my name and told me his was Ron.

We laughed at the shenanigans of people out on the lawn who were dancing to a trio playing a poor rendition of a Beatles tune.

Ron touched my arm and asked, "Are you married?"

"Not anymore," I said. "Are you?"

"Yes," he said. "But neither happily nor forever."

I made no comment.

Garner found me on the balcony and asked if I was ready to leave.

"Yes," I said.

Garner exchanged greetings with Ron.

Garner said, "Janie, you have been having a conversation with Dr. Ron Borne, the university's premier researcher."

"One of many researchers," Ron said, "but certainly not the best."

My children were visiting their father for the week, so I was free to be entertained and escorted by Garner.

The next morning, a Sunday, Garner picked me up. We went to the Beacon for breakfast. While eating grits, biscuits, and coffee, I saw Ron come into the restaurant with another man who looked unkempt.

Ron walked over to our table.

The disheveled man walked up and Garner spoke to him.

"Good morning, Willie Morris," Garner said, "aren't you up mighty early this morning."

"Well, neighbor," Willie said, "I am in fact just finishing up my night."

Garner and Willie lived next door to one another on faculty row.

Garner invited the men to join us. They did. Willie asked me where I had come from.

"Originally Gulfport," I said, "and more recently Mississippi State."

"Aha!" Willie yelled, "We have recruited yet another one. Are you like the others? By leaving Starkville you lowered their general IQ and coming to Oxford you raised the Intelligent Quotient here."

"I don't think so," I replied, not sure of what he meant.

Then Willie qualified it.

"Well if you are related to Mr. Garner James, probably the youngest person to ever graduate from this university, and Dr. Francis James, world renowned archeologist, you must have plenty of brain cells….which my dear is very important here in this intellectually stimulating environment."

I did not know if Willie was being sarcastic or stating a truth.

Ron, who had not taken his eyes off me, asked, "Do you work here?"

"No," I said, "I am applying for a job at the University."

"Oh, which one?"

"It's for an assistant position in the Department of University Affairs."

"Oh, you'll get the job," Willie said. "You'll like working with Robert Khayat."

"Wait a minute." I said. "I don't have the job and in fact have not even been interviewed yet."

Ron stared at me all through breakfast. Soon the conversation ebbed. Garner and I stood up to leave. Ron picked up our bill and followed us to the door.

"Thanks, Ron," we said, simultaneously.

Garner added, "You didn't need to pay for us."

"I hope it is the first of many opportunities to do so."

Ron walked us out to the car and asked me, "Can I call you for dinner some night?"

"Thanks," I said. "That better wait for a more appropriate time."

"Ok," he said, nodding and smiling. "Well, maybe I'll see you around campus."

• • •

In January, I was hired to work as an assistant to Dr. Khayat. His department was charged with improving the image of the university, as well as orchestrating its first private giving campaign.

My professional life became exciting again.

I met people whom Robert invited to the university to encourage them to become donors and to sponsor new programs he wanted developed. One of the programs (designed to put Ole Miss in the media spotlight) was a Visiting Writer's Program. Robert asked Willie to head up the project and invite his friends, well known and up-and-coming writers, to visit Ole Miss.

I was asked to facilitate the program.

Willie had been the youngest editor ever of *Harper's* magazine. Under his leadership, Willie brought writers like George Plimpton, Bill Styron, James Dickey, and Alex Haley to Oxford.

I was fortunate to meet these creative giants. I planned dinners, parties, and speaking engagements for them.

When Alex Haley, author of *Roots*, came to Oxford, football coach Billy Brewer brought the black members of his football team to hear him speak. When one tall, slender, very dark young man came in, Mr. Haley stood up and asked the young man to come forward.

"Son," he said, "I can probably tell you which ancient tribe your people in Africa came from."

"Really?" the young man said, "Who were they?"

"Maybe," Haley replied, "the Tutsi of Rwanda. They were the tallest people in Africa. You are the offspring of princes."

Willie Morris, Cornelia Henry, and me in Oxford

The young man and his teammates were awed as they listened intently to Mr. Haley's descriptions of African people and customs.

Dean Faulkner Wells and her husband Larry hosted a party for visiting writer James Dickey at their home, which is where Faulkner had written *Absolom, Absolom*. We had all agreed ahead of time to go to Taylor Grocery for dinner. As we were leaving the party going to our cars, a socialite from Oxford walked up to Mr. Dickey.

"Mr. Dickey," she asked, "Would you mind if I called you 'James?'"

"You can call me Son of a Bitch," he said, "for all I care."

When we arrived at Taylor Grocery, famous for its fried catfish, hushpuppies, and creamy tartar sauce, the waitress seated us at a long table and placed a bowl of the tartar sauce in the middle of the table.

Mr. Dickey reached his long arms out, pulled the bowl up to his spot at the table, grabbed a spoon, and started eating the tartar sauce.

After a spoonful or two, he pushed it away and announced, "This is the worst soup I've ever tasted in my life!"

A week later we heard the news. Mr. Dickey had been diagnosed with a brain tumor. He was not expected to live.

Since the university faculty members were all invited to the writers' lectures and parties, Ron Borne never missed one. Our visits, as we listened to the chatter from the writers and their entourages, became somewhat of a ritual.

• • •

Ron, a devout Catholic, had made the difficult decision to divorce.

He wanted to remain a good, caring, and involved father and wanted his wife to find a life that pleased her. He made the necessary and generous legal decisions and was divorced soon after his son's wedding.

Once Ron was divorced, we began dating. When Ron was traveling or busy with research, I met Willie for dinner or drinks at the Hoka, the Holiday Inn, or Syd and Harry's. I never rode with Willie. His drinking made him a rather unreliable driver.

But Willie was a good, caring friend to me and my children. He wrote articles for my son Neil's fledgling local newspaper, *The Oxford Times*. Willie asked Liz to sing for his friends at evening gatherings. He sat with young Jamie at football games. And he encouraged Harry in his quest to be a classical saxophonist.

Neil III married his girlfriend Linda in November of 1985. The next month, Ron asked me to marry him.

I accepted.

When Ron shared our marriage plans with his children, the reaction was not what we had hoped. All three of Ron's children were devout Catholics. The idea that their father was divorced had caused emotional outbursts. Those were mild compared to their reaction to another marriage. None of the three wanted to have anything to do with the ceremony, or it seemed, with us. They were displeased about their dad marrying a much-married woman who was also a non-Catholic.

Their unhappiness clouded our own joy.

My children were non-verbal about the marriage, probably because they had become accustomed to the idea of changing fathers.

Harry was enthralled with Ron's youngest daughter, Meribeth. He was delighted to include her in his extended family. Jamie liked Ron because he could talk about sports. Ron took Jamie to games and bought him Ole Miss shirts and jackets.

Liz was just getting comfortable in Oxford, thoroughly relieved not to have a step-father anymore. When I told her of the upcoming marriage, she cried.

"Mom, I love you," Liz said, crawling into my lap. "You are smart in so many ways. But you have terrible taste in men. Please don't let this be another mistake!"

I promised her I would do my best.

At my fourth wedding with Ron Borne

"Your best may not be enough," she said.

The wedding was in my home. No Catholic church would host the event.

We asked our friend, Municipal Judge Dwight Ball, to officiate.

The wedding was a casual late afternoon affair. Our friends came bearing food, drinks, and gifts. Everyone dressed informally. Even I, the bride, wore slacks and a sweater.

Dwight, who wore a robe to officiate, recalled, "Hell, I was the only one there in a dress."

Our musical friends took turns playing on our upright piano. We sang old songs. If we forgot the words, Willie Morris filled them in. He never forgot anything.

My sister Harriet drove up for the wedding. Ron's brother Allen and his wife came from Minnesota. Harriet caught the flu the day before the wedding. But I knew it really was another type of illness. I felt she was sick with worry and concern for me and my offspring. Harriet treated my children as though they were her very own.

The wedding party lasted nearly all night. But Ron's family left immediately after the vows were spoken. Harriet stayed the night with my children.

Ron and I went to the Holiday Inn for the night. But we came home early the next morning to get ready for Christmas with my children and Neil's new wife Linda.

My children always celebrated Christmas with me a day early. They spent Christmas Eve through New Year's Day with their father.

• • •

On Mother's Day, 1986, I received a handmade card from Harry.

He addressed the envelope to me, with all my prior names written on it — *Mrs. Dr. Jane Ann Stanley White Lovitt Lovitt Borne.*

The message read,

> *Fathers may come and fathers may go,*
> *but you're the only mother I'll ever know.*
> *Love, Harry*

29

Ron, a professor of Medicinal Chemistry in the School of Pharmacy, inspired his students and taught thousands of them over his decades at Ole Miss. He was popular with students and was selected Outstanding Teacher of the Year.

Ron and I were married, but we were also friends. It suited us both.

I enjoyed Ron's company because of his wide range of interests. He was a renaissance man. He studied opera, read literature and poetry, and attended theater. He served on the University's Athletics Committee and attended nearly every football, baseball, and basketball game regardless of where it was being played.

Ron and I enjoyed our years at Ole Miss. Our friends, Charles and Cornelia Henry, David and Lib Sansing, Kay and Warner Alford, Larry and Dean Faulkner Wells, Ken and JoAnn McGraw, Willie Morris, and others enriched our lives with laughter, love and meaning.

The sports, dinners together, and conversations were some of the most intriguing and compelling I had ever participated in. On Friday evenings a group of us would share stories of our history, mixed with political issues, over catfish at Taylor Grocery. Sometimes the fare was a bit fancier in restaurants on the Oxford square, but the conversation was just as rich. Sunday afternoons we played Trivial Pursuit. During each game, our goal was to find a single question Willie could not answer. It rarely happened.

In September of 1986, Linda gave birth to Neil Ware White IV.

Working for Ole Miss in the mid-1980s

Ron became a grandfather. He embraced this role and took baby Neil on trips to Disney World and Epcot Center. The two, one tall, the other short, were intrigued with each other. In the end zone at one of the Ole Miss football games after Ron had bought Neil IV popcorn, cokes, baseball caps, and anything else he wanted, Dr. David Sansing proclaimed to the South End Zoners, "when I come back after death, I want to be Ron Borne's grandson."

• • •

I agreed to attend the Catholic Church on University Avenue with Ron. I wanted to be a supportive wife. We usually attended the 5:00 afternoon service.

I enjoyed the quiet of the afternoon service, but had a difficult time understanding the priest. Either his voice was not loud enough or the address system was out of order, but I seldom heard a complete homily.

Ron was pleased that I made the effort to be with him.

One evening after returning from mass, Ron asked me if I would be willing for him to have my marriages annulled. I wasn't particularly thrilled with the idea. In fact, I thought it irrelevant and unnecessary.

"Ron," I asked, "would that mean my children would be 'bastards'? 'Illegal?'"

"Yes," he said. "But that is church law if they are to recognize our marriage."

I struggled with my response.

"Go ahead if you must," I said, "but it doesn't sound like such a good idea to me."

A few weeks later Ron came home from work later than usual. When he walked in the door, he had a stack of papers about six inches tall in his hands. He threw the stack on the table.

"What's the matter?" I asked.

"These are all the papers you have to fill out about all of your marriages — the one to Neil; the two to John."

He paused and sat down in a kitchen chair. He stretched his arms out on the table and stared out the window.

"Ron, you ok?"

"No," he said, "hell no!" He shook his head in disbelief. "The church suggested a $10,000 donation might make the annulments more feasible."

"Oh, my Gosh!" I said. "I'm sorry. I had no idea you had to pay for them."

"Well, I'm not going to. It's more of the same...money greasing palms whether in politics or church. I'm tired of it all."

We still attended the Catholic Church, but less seldom. He dropped out of the men's group he once belonged to.

As I'm prone to do, I felt responsible. I believed it was my fault that he was becoming less of a church member. Nothing seemed easy in this relationship.

I also felt badly about a promise I made to Jamie. When I told Jamie we were going to move across town into Ron's house, Jamie asked, "How will I get to Sunday School? I can walk from here, but you'll have to drive me if we move out by the Country Club."

I assured Jamie I would be happy to take him each Sunday. Some Sundays I did. On others, I did not. Other days, Jamie said he did not want to go.

• • •

My other three children thought I loved Harry best. I suppose that's because Harry and I seldom had conflicts. He listened to and played music whenever he wasn't at school or doing something else that was required of him. As a fourteen year old he got a job as a dishwasher in the restaurant next door to our house so he could practice his saxophone after the restaurant closed. The rest of us verbally supported Harry in his love of music, but in practice we often wished his horn were quieter!

His commitment to his music paid off. Years later he received a full music scholarship to the University of Southern Mississippi (USM).

Harry was delightful. When his music professor at the University of Southern Mississippi asked how Harry got such an unusual middle name — Kinross — I recounted the story of Harry being conceived in Kinrosshire, Scotland.

Quick as a flash, Harry said, "Yeah, and my little sister's middle name is 'Motel Six.'"

Harry brought friends home from USM for the weekend, all attractive, fun, and pleasant people. His sophomore year, he came home one afternoon to get his laundry done. I was in my bedroom reading. He came to the door and said he needed to talk to me. I was alone because Ron was in Scotland for a year-long sabbatical.

"Ok, Harry, come sit by me and tell me what's on your mind."

He was hesitant, unusual for verbally quick Harry. I waited.

"Mom, I don't think you are going to like what I tell you."

"Ok, so tell me. What's the problem?"

"It's not a problem for me any longer but I think it will be for you."

He paused and then said, "I'm gay."

I looked at his handsome face, his large hands that so skillfully played the alto sax. I listened to his voice which had a tone of joyful seriousness. I never quite knew when Harry was teasing. However, I felt the gravity in his voice.

I thought of all the ways I should respond. I thought of all the grandbabies, his babies. I had looked forward to expanding my gene pool through Harry. Now that was not to be. I said, "Harry, are you sure? You've brought home beautiful young girls that were your girlfriends, who seemed to love you. Are you sure?"

"Yes, Mom, I am sure. It was those beautiful girls who helped me acknowledge my true sexuality."

Again I paused. I thought for long minutes. I took his hands and asked, "Will you do me a favor? If this is who you are you know I will love you no matter what. But because I do care and would like some reassurance, would you go see a counselor or a doctor and at least talk to one?"

"Mom, that's not necessary. But if it will make you feel better, ok. Who do you want me to see?

I had a Christian friend whose husband was a psychiatrist, who also professed to be Christian. I asked Harry to call him for an appointment. He did.

Three days later Harry came in, sat next to me, put his arms around me, and said, "What a waste of time!"

I asked, "What happened? What did he say?"

"He asked me lots of questions. Then he told me to get on my knees, ask God to forgive me for my sin of my impure sexual orientation. He said the Bible calls it an abomination. I told him I did not choose this orientation. It was my natural self."

"Oh, Harry. I am so sorry. I regret I sent you to him."

Harry replied, "Well, he did tell me something interesting. He said all human sexuality is on a continuum from 0 to 100. He said most homosexuals range in the 20 to 50 range and most heterosexuals from 50 to 90. No one is ever one-hundred percent homosexual or hetero. I thought that was interesting."

Harry was a devout Christian, enjoyed church, and was biblically knowledgeable. I thought he might find difficulty fitting in traditional southern churches.

"Don't worry, Mom," he said. "God doesn't read the same Bible fundamental thinkers and believers read." With that statement, he got up, hugged me, and said, "I've got to drive back to Hattiesburg. Our band has a concert tonight. Love you."

When Harry left that afternoon, I got on my bed, put the pillow over my head so I could not see anything. My stomach ached. It almost felt like the son I knew had disappeared. Would he be different? Would he act strange? Would he behave in ways that would endanger him? The gay community was in the midst of the AIDS crisis and no cure was in sight.

I needed reassurance that the world had not stopped and Harry had not gotten off. I got up and turned on my music. Sinatra's "My Way" usually had an inspiring effect on me. It opened my brain to possibilities I never thought about at other times. My way? My way? But this time all I could think about was Harry's way? Dear God, why? I turned the music off and sat in silence. I was concerned for him. I questioned my own ability to cope with this revelation of Harry's. He had always been different from others. Not feminine but caring, loving, and sensitive beyond his years. I knew this was a time I needed to avoid self-pity and panic, and absolutely avoid judging or condemning him. I loved him. But I didn't want him to change in drastic ways. At least not so suddenly. I couldn't help it. I went into full mother-worry, grief and dismay.

What would become of this talented, caring young man who had such high hopes for his place in the world? What kind of conflict would he find, or worse, what kind of prejudice would he face? And would he be able to handle the issues that were sure to arise?

I tried to reason with myself, "Perhaps the music world, the artistic venues, might be the places he finds acceptance, creativity, companionship, and hopefully even love. But I did not know. How could I know? How could I best help Harry, or at least support him? There were so many pitfalls. I did not want to fall into one and lose him. I prayed, and cried, and was so frustrated with not knowing I stayed in bed all afternoon, reluctant to get up and face a world that had turned on its side.

My desire was for him to have a family, a loving wife, and babies. I grieved for the loss of those possibilities. I screamed at myself, "My God, I am so selfish. Worried about me. What is my child going through? Then I thought about something Harry told me when he was about twelve years old.

In Harry's early years he was dyslexic, wore eyeglasses, was left-handed, and awkward. I was an over-protective mother. I excused my over-protection of him because I had to be mother — and oftentimes father — to him. I refused to allow Harry certain privileges for fear he would be hurt. One afternoon he came and plopped down beside me. He wanted to go to a party with much older teens. I said, "No, no way."

"Why?" he asked.

"I don't trust those young people, or you with them. They drink! They drive too fast. No way. You don't need them!"

"Mom," he said, "your keeping me from living will not keep me from dying!"

"What do you mean?"

"There is a big, interesting world out there and I want to see it, be part of it, experience all sorts of new things, but you don't want me to. You are holding me back. I'll be very careful, I promise, but when my time comes, it will come. I believe that's in God's hands and not yours."

Even as I agonized over Harry's revelation, even though my fear for him was rampant, I remembered that early conversation and took some reassurance from it. However, weeks went by when I thought of little else. How will people treat Harry? Will his gay-ness be a hindrance to all the things he wants to do and be? Will the church accept him? Will his father accept him? These thoughts ran through my mind on a random basis day after day. I had no answers. Except to love him, as always, and let him guide me in this new arena of thought and emotion.

• • •

My boss, Robert Khayat, Vice-Chancellor at Ole Miss, sent me to Jackson to meet an eccentric wealthy woman named Gertrude (Gayle) Costellow Ford. Robert wanted me to ask her to support programs at the University.

Mrs. Ford had made it known she wanted no part of any university.

She had great disdain for humans, but loved dogs. She wanted all her millions to go to humane societies around the country. Mrs. Ford had built a thirteen bedroom, thirteen bathroom house on Eastover Drive in Jackson, Mississippi. She lived with her eleven Chihuahuas. She added four other rooms where her husband and his caretaker lived.

Three other university presidents had approached Mrs. Ford about donating money. She had literally kicked them out of her front door.

I went to Mrs. Ford's front door and rang the doorbell. When she opened it she was wearing only her panties. Nothing else.

Still entertaining the idea I had once been Mary, Queen of Scots, and knowing Mrs. Ford was a Shakespearean scholar, I introduced myself as Queen Marie, recently departed 400 years ago.

She welcomed me with open arms and asked me to have tea with her. In her palatial living room we sat across from each other as she poured our afternoon tea into fragile cups. She did not offer lemon, cream, or sugar. I took a huge swallow, choked, and realized it was straight bourbon! I ended up spending the night with her. She told me her life's story. I went to bed drunker that I ever thought I could be.

Mrs. Ford claimed to be an atheist but had a passionate love for Edward de Vere, the Earl of Oxford, whom she knew to be the real Shakespeare. She could quote nearly all the sonnets, and between each one she told me the story of the sonnets being written by de Vere to his and the virgin Queen Elizabeth's son who was hidden away and given the title "the Earl of Southampton."

Mrs. Ford wrote about her theories in two books, one written in the same style and language the real Shakespeare had used.

I went back to see Mrs. Ford on a regular basis. I often spent the night. She was brilliant, funny, caustic, and, yes, mean as a snake to just about everyone she encountered.

On one of my trips, I took her to a theater to see the movie *Henry*

V. She quoted along with the movie until the actor misspoke. Mrs. Ford jumped up, screamed at the screen, and called the movie producers names that I had heard only from gang members.

She jerked me up and we promptly left the theater.

We became close friends. I did not want her money and I did not care if she gave any to the University. She needed a friend more than any human I had ever met.

She had been a multi-millionaire all of her life. She felt as if no one liked her for herself, her brain, or her personality.

I did.

• • •

Enjoying bourbon in a teacup, a memory surfaced. In 1946, Aunt Vi came on the Hummingbird train from New York to Gulfport. She and I listened to the Jessup Brothers on Radio Station XERF. They broadcast all the way from Del Rio, Texas.

While we listened to the show, Vi laughed, smoked a cigarette, and sipped bourbon out of a coffee cup so Floy wouldn't know she was drinking. Hiding her bourbon was a secret Vi shared with me. I felt special that she told me.

Brother Jessup told his radio audience that if we sent him a five-dollar bill he would mail to us a splinter of wood from the cross of Jesus, a bar of soap to wash away our sins, and a slick black and white photograph of Jesus, personally autographed by Jesus Christ himself.

"Vi," I said, "will you lend me five dollars? I want a picture of Jesus . . . and those other things."

"Janie," she said, "that's a waste of money. There are no such things. Those men are telling a bunch of lies."

"You mean preachers lie?"

"Some of them do."

"Please, please!" I cried, "My birthday is soon. That can be your present to me. Please, Vi." Then I added, "If you help, then I won't tell Floy about that stuff in your coffee cup."

Vi, who seemed amused, said, "You are threatening me, huh? You little weasel. Why is this so important to you?"

"Mama says I have to talk to Jesus every day. If I had his picture it'd be easier to talk to him."

Vi laughed hard. "Ok, kiddo. Let's get an envelope and send off for that load of garbage. And Happy Birthday!"

I met the mailman day after day waiting for my package. After a few weeks, I gave up and yelled at the radio, "You preachers are liars! I hate you!"

A few days after my birthday, the package arrived.

I tore it open. The autographed photo of Jesus fell out. "He" had signed in cursive letters: "To My Dear Friend Jane. Love, Jesus Christ."

I never did get the advertised splinter from the cross or the soap to wash away my sins. But I trusted that looking at His picture would make it easier for me to talk to Jesus. I tacked the photograph of Jesus over my bed. Right next to the one of Roy Rogers and Trigger.

• • •

Ron and I traveled the world. Together, we went to Paris, Scotland, Venice, musicals in London's Soho district, Broadway fare in Memphis, and Saints games in New Orleans. These places sat as comfortably with us as did the pub in New Orleans where Ron grew up. The pub featured Cajun cuisine and walls decorated with the rear ends of stuffed African bounty. On one trip to Venice we wanted to attend an opera. As we stood in the St. Mark's Square trying to read a map, a dapper Italian gentleman stopped to ask if he could be of help. Ron told him we were looking for La Fenice, the ancient, elegant opera house. The gentleman introduced himself as Senator Primoli. He walked with us to Teatro La Fenice and helped us purchase tickets to "Rigoletto," even though it was sold out that night.

Ron and I also shared a love of Scotland. Perhaps that was our greatest bond.

On one of our many trips to Edinburgh, I started to piece together what I believed about God.

I hungered for a lightness in my soul. I had tried so many religious denominations. I grew up thinking the Baptist God was spelled *Gawd*. The dogma, damnation, and judgment didn't sit well with me. But as a Baptist I did learn to memorize scripture. And, of course, I kept my autographed photo of Jesus on my wall.

I spent time as a Methodist. As the name implies, Methodists are methodical in their belief about an accepting, loving God. Their view of God was far too specific for me.

Presbyterians provided me with friendship and encouragement, but with a doctrinal formula for faith.

I attended an Episcopal church and found the Prayer Book poetic. I even ventured briefly into Catholicism, occasionally illegally sampling the transubstantiated body and blood of Jesus.

These denominations and others serve God in their own way, yet each seemed to rely on the fact that to "get to heaven you had to believe Jesus died for your sins."

I had a difficult time worshipping a God purported to be all loving and forgiving, yet who would ordain the murder of a holy human being for someone else to achieve an eternal blessing.

I wanted to feel the presence of the sacred in all of life. I craved a God and a fellowship that simply loved all of me all of the time no matter what mistakes I made or sins I committed. I had no name for the God of my yearning other than the traditional names. I prayed many times day and night. But to whom? Not to the God defined and owned by some traditional southern religions. I desired a personal relationship with God that transcended the confining and limited versions of Him previously taught to me.

I wanted a God who was an ever unfolding mystery, rather than one defined by creeds and dogma. When I prayed under a full moon on the Gulf or on Scotland's Blackford Hill, I felt connected, like I was experiencing an, intimate candlelight conversation. That feeling was euphoric and lasted well past the waning of the moon.

In my search for something that could provide the completeness I desired, I knew religiosity and spirituality were two very different experiences. It was not a religious, institutionalized denomination I needed. I needed an unconstrained, unlimited, spirituality. Once that idea came to me, I thought Celtic spirituality may be my future. I stumbled upon the Celtic phenomenon of thin places and thin times...places and moments when there is a thin line between heaven and earth, between the God of Creation and the God of me. The secular and holy blended into one spirituality. These thin moments, no matter where we are actually standing, are times when we experience unexpected emotional ecstasy, spiritual enlightenment, and a peace that is found inside us.

When we are aware that there is something larger and more enduring than ourselves, yet an intricate part of us as well, we are in a thin place.

Celtic spirituality is a spiritual mind rather than a specific religion. Celtic Christianity, which grew out of ancient Celtic spirituality, sees God in every human being, every living creature, and every plant, flower, and tree. God is also in sunrises and sunsets, clouds, thunder and lightning, and in both the best and worst of us. Celtic Christians worship God in nature at its loveliest as well as its most threatening form. To Celtic Christians all moments and all places are sacred.

Rather than being a Presbyterian, Methodist, Baptist, or Episcopalian Christian I am akin to the early believers known as Celtic Christians who saw God and the risen Christ in all of life and a spark of the divine in all human life. When I know, feel, and understand an Almighty Presence within me and all around me, I am secure in a cocoon of spiritual and emotional safety. And in those moments, I am transformed.

Being inspired by Celtic Christianity led me to re-think the place Jesus of Nazareth has in my belief system. Many churches where I have worshipped seemed to focus on the death and resurrection of Jesus. I focus on his life. He loved life. He loved people. He loved his God in a familial way, calling him "Abba" meaning "Daddy." He wanted all people to have this intimacy with the God of all creation. Jesus lived to help people be open to a healthy and meaningful life. He lived a life of holy strength, which was amazing because he was a wandering, itinerant teacher without a home. He was marginalized because he had no interest in wealth and political power. He was considered an outcast because he touched lepers, befriended prostitutes, and rebelled against the rigorous Jewish laws that hindered freedom. He specifically taught that all people have a direct access to God without needing priests or sacrifices. Both the Roman and Jewish hierarchies felt threatened by his teachings. They despised him.

It was in his humanity that he rose to the level of rabbi and healer. His faith showed others they could likewise practice unconditional love and forgiveness, both of which are life-changing. On a daily basis Jesus lived his teachings while he was on earth. His spirit still resides in these wisdom lessons making him and the values he taught universal and eternal.

Jesus is my Person, the one I think of with great spiritual joy and gratitude. He is my inspiration. His resurrection is real to me every time I do a loving act, share, forgive, or serve. His risen-ness woos me to be more like he was during his physical time, while his vibrant spirit enlivens and animates me. He often saves me from myself. He is my Lord, my model for living, and the source of my peace and security.

Back on Blackford Hills in Edinburgh, at the same spot where I felt the first call to ministry in 1969, I pondered depths of life, my own being within its endless circle.

I marvel at the incalculable mystery of it all. I was once a tiny one-celled creature and look at me now. God lives within.

At moments like these, holiness seemed normal.

30

When my uncle Garner died and left instructions to be cremated and have his ashes scattered in Maldon, England, I was dismayed. My sister Harriet suggested dumping the ashes in the Gulf with the hope that in some distant day the Gulf Stream would eventually float them to the Maldon area. I couldn't agree to that, which meant I was the one who would have to do the scattering.

My son Harry lived in Germany so I thought perhaps he would be willing to do the deed for me. I called to tell him Uncle Garner might be coming in the mail to him. He discouraged my mailing Uncle Garner for fear the ashes might be mistaken for illegal drugs. Harry did agree, though, to meet me in England and help with the ultimate dispersal of Uncle Garner's ashes.

Ron came to my rescue. He was headed to Scotland for a research project, so he toted Uncle Garner across the Atlantic in his golf bag. We met in the middle of the British Isles. He brought Garner to me, then he went north toward Edinburgh and I went south to Maldon.

Harry and I met in London. We left the Liverpool Street train station on the 9:02 to Chelmsford, England. Ever the one to overdo ethics, Harry thought we ought to buy a ticket for Uncle Garner. I snarled at him. With Uncle Garner, carefully packaged and hidden under my arm, we disembarked from the train.

Walking through Chelmsford station, we stopped to purchase one long-stemmed red rose for this sacred occasion. My son was carrying his saxophone and I was carefully balancing Uncle Garner, the long red rose, and my Amplified New Testament.

As only divine guidance can produce, the Chelmsford bus station was only a few feet away from the flower stall. We quickly boarded the Number 31 bus to Maldon. After twenty-five minutes of riding through the villages of Essex we arrived at our destination. Gathering our belongings, we asked the bus driver to direct us to St. Mary's The Virgin Church, which was adjacent to the Jolly Sailor Pub. It was a brief walk down a rose-lined lane to the tidal marshes of the Blackwater River, which runs inland from the North Sea.

We walked along the quay admiring the huge sailing barges with towering masts. This sight of giant orange sails moving bulky barges down river was a sensory stimulation — a scene from a Monet painting.

Four years earlier, almost to the day, Uncle Garner embarked on his own journey to Maldon. His wife Frances Theiss James had passed away.

Frances was a prestigious archaeologist/anthropologist who served as Professor of Anthropology at Ole Miss for several years. Her prior life was one of academic achievement. Frances was a Phi Beta Kappa graduate of Bucknell University. Her mother died when Frances was an infant. Her father, Dr. Lewis Theiss, Professor of Journalism, instead of hiring a caretaker, took Frances with him to Bucknell. She spent her youth in libraries and classrooms rather than learning to play, socialize, dance or learn the art of "chit chat." Frances was shy, withdrawn, and quiet. All of which made her seem aloof, uncaring and cold. Garner did not see her that way; in fact they had a breathless passion for each other. After Garner died, I found page after page of letters with handwritten intimacies and desires.

After WWII Frances worked as a journalist in England where she and Garner lived. She wrote articles about archaeology and became fascinated by the subject. She pursued it at a frantic pace. Frances received diplomas in the Archaeology of Roman Provinces, Iron Age Europe, and

Archeology of Western Asia.

In 1963 she received a Ph.D. in Palestinian Archaeology at the University of London's Institute of Archaeology. She studied and worked with such giants of archaeology as Dame Kathleen Kenyon, Sir Mortimer Wheeler, and V. Gordon Chide. She helped "dig up" the Iron Age of Beth Shan, that village where King Saul's enemies cut off his head and fastened his body to the wall. Frances wrote a Monograph for the University of Pennsylvania that amassed her research.

Garner and Frances spent one halcyon summer in Maldon, England, in a canal side cottage. They spent their time there writing articles for *National Geographic*, and feeding some of the 300 wild swans who lived on the canal. Garner and Frances saw the swans, which mate for life, as kindred souls. Both Garner and Frances had expressed the desire to reside in that spot for all eternity. Frances' unexpected death from heart failure was a blow to Garner. His wife was his passion. His identity, to a large extent, came from being Frances' husband. He, the extrovert, dreamer, dancer, visionary, creator, and inventor, was enthralled with the words, thoughts, and writings that came from his beloved and brilliant wife. Frances donated her body to the university's medical center for research, wanting to teach even beyond her time on earth. After a year, Frances was cremated.

Garner packed his bags with Frances safely stowed inside of one. He purchased a round trip ticket to London on the Queen Elizabeth II and settled in to the ship's social life for a full seven days. On day five, Garner saw on the daily activities list a talent show — and the passengers were to provide the talent.

Garner immediately signed up. The winner was to receive a trophy and a cash gift of 50 English pounds.

Evening came. Garner donned his tight-fitting tuxedo. His tight pants caused a wedgie in his buttocks area. Wanting Frances to look her best, he wrapped the red plastic box of her remains in a lace scarf he had brought along to hold her ashes as he sprinkled them. When he appeared at the talent desk, he received a large number "4" which was pinned to his back.

Prior to Garner's performance, there had been a singer, a piano player, and a couple who did a jazz jig. Then it was Garner's turn. He pranced to the center of the room and instructed the orchestra he was ready for them to begin.

The orchestra played a classical rendition of Johann Strauss II's "The Beautiful Blue Danube." Garner, holding boxed up Frances in his arms, began waltzing, twirling, dipping to the music . . . all the while making eye contact with (and shedding a tear over) his beloved.

When the music stopped, Garner bowed to tremendous applause.

Of course, he won the talent show. Who would vote against a grieving man dancing with his dead wife!

Arriving in Maldon, Harry and I searched for the swans that reportedly have lived on that canal since the days when Richard the Lion Hearted first brought the original pair from the Holy Land. We were sorely disappointed that the now famous swans had disappeared.

Reluctantly we walked back up a steep incline and entered the walled churchyard of St. Mary's The Virgin, built in the 1100s. Wild flowers decorated ancient tombstones and multitudes of floral blossoms colored the grey stone church in memory, today, of the Battle of Maldon, fought in 991 A.D. on this site. The locals referred to this event as the 'millennium.'

Ambling over the church grounds, we found a lone pine tree standing as a stately sentinel over the remains of men who had fought and died a thousand years before the Norman invasion of 1066 and where they had been laid to rest. Harry assembled his saxophone, I unwrapped the red rose, and found the scriptural passage I wanted.

Then we began to unpack Uncle Garner. The white outer box in which he was mailed from the crematory was relatively easy to remove. How-

Harry spreading Garner's ashes at Maldon

ever, the maroon plastic urn was a more difficult matter. In exasperation, we searched for a sharp object, but had to rely on a ballpoint pen with which to pry off the sealed lid.

Harry managed to open the urn about an inch. Something very white popped out! Squealing and jumping back, I feared that Uncle Garner's bones were loose in there! We were relieved to discover it was packing Styrofoam.

Finally, the lid popped free, we emptied the remaining Styrofoam into my purse and Harry pulled out the heavy plastic bag of ashes. Neither of us were comfortable with our task, but we bravely continued on the course we had set for ourselves. Looking at the chips of bone interspersed with ashes, I realized I could not bear to put my hands into the bag to sprinkle the ashes, and I didn't feel it appropriate to just dump them. Graciously, Harry offered to do the sprinkling. We stepped closer together under the waving boughs of the pine tree. As Harry shoveled his hand into the bag and began to sprinkle Uncle Garner around the base of the pine I read the comforting words from Hosea, then Paul and yes, Shakespeare, "Death is swallowed up in victory through our Lord Jesus Christ."

Being a windy day, some of Uncle Garner was blown onto Harry's pants and shoes. Harry quickly brushed off his hands and clothes, picked up his saxophone, and played a mournful, poignant rendition of "Amazing Grace." I listened with eyes closed and head bowed to the high, trilling notes. They seemed to remain clear even as the wind carried them over the watery estuary. When the hymn ended, I placed the long-stemmed red rose amongst the white and grey ashes and prayerfully praised God for life here and now, and for life eternal.

Harry packed away his horn and I stashed the empty urn and mailer in the trash bin and dumped the Styrofoam out of my purse. Solemnly, we walked out of the ancient churchyard toward the quaint Jolly Sailor Pub next door to have a final toast to Uncle Garner. Just as we stepped out of the walled church garden and looked toward the canal, two large, peaceful swans — wings tenderly touching each other — floated by, both of them nodding their heads as though putting their approval on our celebratory ceremony.

With blurred vision we watched them swim behind the wind filled sails of a giant barge until both were out of sight.

• • •

In 1989 Neil and Linda left Oxford and moved to the Mississippi Gulf Coast. Their second child Maggie was born. I had a grandson and a new granddaughter who both lived 300 miles away.

I was also concerned for Jamie. He was an unhappy young man. He despised the schools in Oxford. He had few real friends. He often seemed depressed or distraught. I decided to rent an apartment in Gulfport and move back there to enroll Jamie in the Coast Episcopal Private high school.

I convinced Robert Khayat that I could manage my fundraising duties from the Coast

Jamie's class had only eleven students. There he became involved in basketball, football, and social life. He seemed more content and happier. I could not afford the steep tuition, so I paid half and wrote grants for the school to pay for the remainder.

Ron, who had been spending a sabbatical year in Scotland, stayed in touch by phone. He called every Wednesday morning at 6 a.m. my time and we talked for nearly an hour each time. He also wrote weekly letters almost like a journal. I kept them all.

But I felt like I needed to be on the Coast . . . and that Ron and I could manage a long-distance relationship.

My son Neil, who was only 29 years old, was building a magazine empire. He'd garnered national attention and awards for his magazines. He launched *Coast* magazine, the first full-color glossy publication for the Mississippi Coast. The following year he purchased a fledgling business publication and re-branded it *Coast Business Journal*. He started an advertising agency for for-profit colleges and universities. He developed a custom publishing division. And, at the age of 31, he purchased *Louisiana Life* magazine for $1.2 million.

Something deep inside me felt uneasy about this high-flying, fast-growing business, but everyone from bankers to investors seemed convinced he was doing something special.

I invested $200,000 I had inherited from my Aunt Vi.

I worried about Neil burning out. But there was one silver lining to my son being consumed by his business. While he worked and traveled — and while Neil and Linda fulfilled the demands of their social schedule — I had the joy of keeping my grandchildren.

On April 9, 1992, Neil and I sat on the back porch of the home once owned by Floy and Papa. He told me the business was going under. Then he told me he had been kiting checks to keep the business going. It was illegal.

At the age of 31, my first born son — and the father of my two grandchildren — was facing prison.

31

While son Neil awaited an FBI investigation, trial, and sentencing, he moved his family to New Orleans. They rented an older house on Soniat, a block from the New Orleans streetcar lines. He was appointed as publisher of *New Orleans* magazine.

I found it odd that he would be offered the position considering he was under such legal scrutiny.

"Mom, the governor of Louisiana has been indicted four times," he said. "I don't think anyone in this state cares."

Eventually, Neil pled guilty to one count of bank fraud and Judge Walter Gex sentenced him to 18 months in federal prison.

For several years, I had kept a small courtyard apartment on Toulouse Street in the French Quarter. The room had once been the kitchen for a large house in front. I went to the apartment to write and to spend an occasional fun weekend. After Neil's sentencing, I rented a much larger second floor apartment in the same French Quarter complex. To help Linda with Neil IV and Maggie, I rented them an apartment on the third floor, right above mine. They left their home on Soniat.

They became French Quarter residents.

• • •

The dawn woke me. Craving light, I slept with windows open, free from curtains of any kind. I crawled out of bed, climbed through the large living room window to step out on the balcony. Toulouse Street in the heart of the French Quarter was damp from the early morning dew. Street sweepers were pushing debris to the sides of the road for the garbage truck to scrape up. Inebriated tourists stumbled down the street. I climbed back in the room and turned on the coffee pot. While I showered and dressed I shook with the all-too familiar anxiety that had haunted me for months. Stress held me together like a girdle. My breath was shallow. I was excited to make this trip. But I was also afraid.

I climbed the steps to the third floor apartment to get grandson Neil and granddaughter Maggie. They were making this difficult trip with me. Linda, son Neil's wife, had the children dressed and ready. The three of us held hands, walked down the three flights of stairs, and walked two blocks down Chartres Street to the car park. I tightened them in the back seat of my gray pickup truck, talking to them all the while about going to see their daddy at camp. A psychologist told their father to call the place where he was "camp" instead of "prison."

Three year old Maggie repeated in a sing song voice, "I want my daddy. I want to see my daddy." Six year old Neil sat quietly, looking out the window. I stopped at McDonald's for orange juice and cinnamon rolls for the children and more coffee for me. Then we crossed the spillway and headed north where my son Neil was sentenced to a federal prison which shared space with the Hansen's Disease Hospital. The leprosarium and prison were located in Carville, Louisiana. With each passing mile, my muscles became more rigid. I grabbed the steering wheel so tightly my knuckles were white. It was a month ago that Neil entered the prison for an eighteen-month sentence for kiting checks. He had tried to keep his publishing company viable by doing creative financing. It was his downfall, and the fall was steep.

Today was my first visit. As we rode to the prison, I fretted with recurring questions. Was Neil depressed? Would he be unkempt or appear down-trodden? Would he be happy to see me? I knew he would be thrilled over the sight of his children. But his mom? I just didn't know. Emotions of love for him, my golden boy, mingled with guilt. Could I have been a better mother and prevented his crime? Insecurity floated in among the love, shame. Would he ever recover his spirit of *joie de vivre* or his passion for new ideas and their creations? Would he forever be looked at as a criminal rather than the caring, strong man he was? Questions wouldn't stop. Fear clouded my thinking and I wanted to be empty of feeling.

Then, I remembered my uncle Garner.

Garner was in the Biloxi Regional hospital for more tests. He had colon cancer. He called me early one morning and asked in his high, sweet voice if I could find time for a brief visit with him. "Jane, I have some news for you."

"News?" I asked. "Well is it good news or bad news?"

"Neither," he replied. "It is just news."

"Can't you tell me now?"

"No, I would like to see you."

"Ok, well, can I bring you something? Food? Cookies? Clothes?"

"No, thanks. I have everything I need. The hospital staff is pleasant. My needs are few."

"Ok, then. I can come about two o'clock today."

"Perfect," he said. "I'll see you then."

When I came into his green hospital room he was sitting up in bed reading a *National Geographic* magazine. He remembered with affection his Frances being a contributing writer to the magazine.

"Hi, Jane," he said with a big smile on his face. "Come sit by me," patting the bed.

I did as he asked. For a minute he just looked at me. Then he took my hand in both of his. "Well, I have some news, like I told you."

"Yes. I'm eager to hear it."

"Well, it's just news. Neither good nor bad. Just news," he reiterated.

"What is it?

"My oncologist has given me only days to live, maybe two weeks at the most. Cancer is all through me."

"Garner," I gasped, "that's terrible news! You have so much more to do and give. That can't be right."

"Janie," he said. "Hear me out."

When my family wanted my attention they called me either Janie or Jane Ann. So I knew he was serious.

"Emotions are gifts to us," he explained, "but they do not, absolutely do not, have to be attached to every life event. Some things are just natural happenings that can be received with peace and calmness. This is one of those events."

"Garner, you are talking about life! Of course I'm going to have feelings."

"But negative feelings aren't necessary," he said. "I have lived an exciting, adventurous life. Saw the world. Had parents who supported me when they probably shouldn't have. Loved my wife passionately. Danced with hundreds of beauties. And have two nieces who will carry on our family's traditions of living outside the boxes of society's expectations."

"I don't know what to say," I told him. I paused and added, "I am sad about losing you."

"Don't be. When I'm gone have a party. No church. No preacher. Invite my friends to the top of the bank at the Southern Club and serve champagne and *petit fours*. Tell Harry I would like him to play the sax and Liz to sing. Ask Neil and Jamie to do the eulogy. And you be the gracious host. Laugh, talk, and know I'm still with you, just in another life form."

I took a deep breath. I didn't know what to say. He seemed so calm, assured. We were silent for a few minutes. I knew his distaste for current racially divided southern churches, but I finally managed to ask, "How is your soul?"

He laughed. "My soul is good to go."

Six days later, I hosted a party at the Southern Club. Many of Garner's Gulfport friends flocked to the party. My friends June and Peggy were the pall bearers. They carried the trays of champagne and petit fours. My four children handled the music and the stories honoring their great uncle. Laughter ruled the day.

We felt Garner's lightness all around us.

My thoughts returned to the road and to our prison visit. I wondered which son I might see? I prayed there would be laughter with his children. That he would be upbeat and not sad or morose. But then I thought again about Garner's message to me. I knew I couldn't force Neil to feel or not feel. I could only make emotional decisions for myself. And today I didn't want any emotion except joy, or maybe relief.

We approached the prison. The campus was covered with live oaks and sprawling green spaces. The screened porches gave this place such a southern plantation look I almost forgot it was a prison.

The children were impatient.

"Let me out," shouted Maggie. "I want to see my daddy."

Neil IV was less eager, a bit apprehensive.

I took his hand, looked at him and said, "It's ok. Your daddy is excited about seeing you. Let's go."

He nodded his head. "Ok. Let's go."

We walked down the long hall to the desk where we were scanned with the metal detector. A guard walked us to the family visiting room. Maggie found a table close to the vending machines and Neil went straight to the coke machine. We bought goodies and sat down to wait. I was battling my desire not to be emotional, but the emotions were winning.

Then, the doors were unlocked. Dozens of green clad, booted prisoners came through the doors. They hurried as they walked down the wooden ramp toward the visitor's room. I watched for my son. When I saw him I could not hold back the tears. He came through the door laughing, nudging the prisoner next to him. I noticed his prison uniform was pressed with a crease, his shirttail tightly tucked in, and long hair slicked back. He stood tall, his shoulders back, and he moved toward us with grace. It had been months since I had seen him this handsome or this relaxed.

When he came through the visitors' door, the children spotted him. They ran, shoving chairs out of the way. Both jumped into his arms at the same time. The hugs seemed endless. I waited patiently for my turn. Neil carried both children over to me, sat them down. I stood up to hug him, drying my tears on his shirt so he wouldn't see them.

Smiling, he said in his usual clipped way, "Hi, Mom. Thanks for coming, for bringing Neil and Maggie. I love you!"

I moved away to a corner of the room to spend the morning watching the playful, loving reunion happening at their table and outside on the playground. I had often wondered what unconditional love looked like. I not only saw it that day, I experienced it. And I imagined, for them, it was a moment the Celts would describe as "thin."

Too soon, visiting hours were over. With goodbye hugs and promises to return next visiting day, the children headed toward the exit. When I opened the door, I turned back to look at Neil. He was watching me. Neither of us even tried to hide the few tears that clouded our eyes. The children and I slowly walked outside and reluctantly climbed back in the truck to start back home.

"Good visit," I said.

Neither child responded.

Five miles down Highway 141 Maggie wailed, "I want my daddy."

Neil IV said, "I want a hamburger."

I drove down River Road in silence. Soon the children napped and I relived the day.

Even now, I remember it as a moment of high achievement, an acme of human resilience.

32

Ron returned from his year abroad in Scotland. I knew I was needed in two places. One with Ron in Oxford and one with my son's children in New Orleans. I spent nearly every weekend on the road, either to take the children to see Neil, or to Oxford to spend time with Ron. Weekdays I spent taking Neil IV to Trinity — a private school that Ron had generously paid for — and Maggie to attend the three-year-old program at Louise McGehee School.

Ron drove down from Oxford to attend Grandparent's Day at Neil's school and to continue creating lasting bonds with his grandson Neil IV.

Most days after school, Neil and Maggie joined me to have afternoon teas, stroll through the Quarter to Jackson Square, or to stop for ice cream at the shop on Pirate's Alley. Most nights I cooked supper for Linda and the children.

The reunions with Ron either in New Orleans or Oxford were strained. I knew he wanted me with him all the time. Part of me wanted that, too. Another part of me wanted that year with Neil and his children. As creative, intelligent, and free-thinking as Ron was about most things, he was traditional in regard to relationships, especially ours. He wanted a stay-at-home wife to clean, keep the house organized, cook, and entertain whenever he desired. He also wanted me to dress up and look professionally acceptable at all times.

I wanted to be up and doing. I had stabled one of my horses outside of Oxford and as often as possible escaped to ride, galloping up and down the red clay hills and through dried creek beds.

Ron, never willing to admit defeat or failure in any way, pretended all was well with us.

He was as supportive of me as he could be in external ways, yet he was unhappy with me and our long-distance situation.

Our relationship limped along in sporadic bursts of togetherness.

When Neil had been in prison for about six months, Linda divorced him, packed up the children, and moved back to Oxford. Ron assumed I would immediately move back to Oxford, too.

I chose to stay in New Orleans.

Ron filed for divorce.

I had many regrets. I loved Ron in many ways. We had enjoyed good times together. I felt there was a kinship between us that would last forever, at least in some way. I wrote a series of poems to him, remembering both the happy and the sad times. I named it *One Song*, printed a hard copy for him, and sent it to him.

After the divorce was final, he came to New Orleans with a lady friend and they stayed in my small apartment. At his request I met him at Café DuMond. He told me he was going to get married. I felt both relief that he had found someone to love, and regret that I could not be that person.

It was a fond and tearful goodbye for both of us.

A HIGHER CONSCIOUSNESS

We went together to one of the highest planes
on this planet,
Mount Pilatus,
to better see the view and valleys below
of fog and haze and snow and green
and frozen cedars
and a chapel on an extended mountain finger.

From that lofty height
over a hot rum punch
I knew there would be
higher planes of consciousness for us to
experience together
but you started back down
while my eyes were still fixed on
the daylight moon.

A poem I wrote in the collection, One Song

33

As part of my job at Ole Miss, I wrote a grant to the Department of Defense to establish a pre-military program to assist high school drop-out students prepare to take the ASVAB test.

I was also approached by the Girl Scouts to work in their program. During the summer of 1994 I worked for the Girl Scouts at Camp Meridale in Meridian. It was primarily a horse camp where we taught girls to care for horses and to trail ride. One morning I was on the deck outside the camp's kitchen. I clumsily turned and fell to the ground about six feet down. I landed on my ankle. I heard it snap and I was in agony.

A carpenter, on the roof repairing shingles, heard my cry, and raced down his ladder.

I was writhing on the ground. He told me to be still, gently pulled off my boot, placed both hands on my ankle. Then he bowed his head and silently prayed.

In a few minutes he stood, picked me up, and drove me to the hospital.

"You probably ought to get an x-ray," he said, "but I know for certain there's nothing wrong with your ankle. You've been healed."

He was true to his word. The doctors said there was no damage.

Driving back to camp, I broke the silence and asked, "How did you do that?"

"I am a carpenter," he said, "like the Lord Jesus. I am also a healer. Jesus healed you using my hands."

He explained he had been called to the ministry while he was a young man in prison. He had spent his youth stealing to survive. At first it was groceries and clothes. Later it was cars and trucks. When his prison sentence ended, he went to Cleveland, Tennessee and enrolled in a seminary at the United Christian Church and Ministerial Association. After he graduated, he became an evangelical minister and moved from town to town getting odd jobs so he could teach and heal.

"The Lord sent me here for you," he said. "Not just to heal your broken ankle but to tell you that you need to go to seminary. The Holy God is waiting for you to do just that."

The next day, I called the United Christian Church's office in Tennessee and inquired about their seminary. Since I had no money to move there, the administrator suggested I take their Biblical Studies Course through correspondence.

That was music to my ears. Individual study was my preferred form of instruction. To complete both the Old and New Testament courses would take me on a two-and-a-half year journey through the Bible, reading and reflecting on nearly every verse.

I worked on the courses at night while I was as Camp Meridale. I studied in my New Orleans apartment. I read and completed assignments at my Gulfport house.

I regularly moved between the apartment in New Orleans and my house in Gulfport. I called the Gulfport house "Vi's house" because Floy and Papa had left it to her. She, in turn, had left it to me. I realized that with all my savings gone, and limited income, I needed to earn some money . . . and reduce expenses.

I decided to let go of the apartments in New Orleans and made the tough decision to rent out my Gulfport house. So I had nowhere to live.

Through all the trauma over the past year — my son's incarceration, my divorce, the loss of my investment income — I had increasingly relied on random blessings from God and His universe to maintain me. Now, more than ever, I needed a miracle.

One day, I received a white envelope with no return address. On the outside, my name, "Jane" was handwritten. No last name. No stamp. Someone had placed it in the mailbox at my friend Gail Cotton's house.

I opened the envelope to find a pre-paid credit card in the amount of $3,000.

I had no idea who sent it. Who could I thank? Should I use it? I kept it in my Bible for several weeks and prayed about its origin and possible use. All the inquiries I made as to where the funds had come from were dead ends. I could not identify my benefactor.

Times were desperate. So I decided to use the funds to make a home for myself. I drove to Shed City, on Highway 49, and ordered a pre-fabricated, 16x24 foot shed to construct in Gail's back yard. The cost was $1,800.

I had enough remaining to install wiring and plumbing in the shed. Gail and I sheet rocked and painted the inside. I put a small, screened porch around the shed, bought a microwave, and a tiny fridge. The porch became my kitchen and dining room, and a place of great camaraderie. Gail and my friend Jo Kennedy came over almost every night to dine with me. We placed candles on the table, cooked "hot plate" pasta, and sprinkled it with olive oil and parmesan cheese. The little fridge cooled bottles of Merlot and Chardonnay. Night after night we three friends sat together sharing our loneliness, our sorrows, but also our joys. We laughed a lot. The time in my shed was peaceful and carefree.

I called this my minimalist period.

One evening Gail, Jo and I were having our usual pasta and salad dinner. We had talked seriously about the future, and specifically our individual futures. I confided in them once again that my desire was to be a teaching minister. I wanted people to connect or re-connect with Biblical stories as allegory which leads them to ultimate truths. Jo responded by sharing her interest. She said, "I love to cook. In fact, that's my favorite thing to do." Laughing, she said to me, "You get folks to listen to you and I will feed them delicious home-cooked meals."

"You two ladies just want to nourish folks," Gail said. "You both are nourishers!"

"Hey," I exclaimed, "When I start my church we can name it The Nourishing Place!"

• • •

That fall of 1995, the Girl Scouts asked me to manage a camp for at-risk children over the holiday period. The session was held at Camp Itikana outside of Wiggins. Thirty-five boys and girls were scheduled to attend. I needed volunteers.

Many friends joined the efforts as camp counselors and cooks. That's where I first met Max Peck. He was manager of the FAA Tower at the Gulfport International Airport. He was also a Sheriff's deputy.

Max and his friend John King volunteered to handle the boys at the camp; Gail, Jo and I managed the girls. Max and I became friends. For the first year of our friendship he never asked me for a date. But at least once a week, we met for lunch. He soon became my best friend.

He, too, enjoyed riding horses. He bought a palomino to share stable space with my horse Traveler. On weekends we rode together through the nature trail in our neighborhood.

I had completed the Biblical Studies Program through the United Christian Church, but still desired further study at a seminary. Then I received another blessing . . . a second miracle.

A rather nondescript business envelope arrived in my post office box. The return address read "The Gertrude C. Ford Foundation." Inside was a check from Mrs. Ford's estate. It was made out to me — in the amount of $135,000.

I used the funds to pay off all my debts (including old debts from my marriage to John), paid for Liz's college, and had enough left over for seminary tuition and travel.

I immediately contacted Columbia Presbyterian Seminary in Decatur, Georgia and signed up for their Spiritual Development program.

This was a program for working adults, not typical young, full-time seminarians. We went to courses one week a month with prescribed readings and papers required after each course. One of the courses was held at the Monastery of the Holy Spirit at Conyers, Georgia.

Except for class time, it was a silent retreat.

That entire week, I felt the pull: an undeniable confronting of the idea that I wanted to be clergy...not so much a preacher as a teacher.

I had felt the call before, but having been divorced several times and having to support four children as a single mother, I didn't think I could say *yes* to God. My faith wasn't strong, otherwise I would have known that God would take care of my needs. In retrospect, I experienced pain and struggles that made me more humble, more understanding of the trials of others. My golden boy Neil III went to prison; my musical, kind, and sweet boy Harry admitted to being gay; my lovely and gifted daughter, longing for a empathetic adult male, could not build stable relationships with boys; and my youngest son Jamie dove into an early dependence on alcohol.

I learned first-hand the pain of a mother who loved too much and disciplined too little. But I knew deep down that those tough days would make me a better, more understanding person.

At this retreat we had an assignment: Write a paragraph describing a barrier between you and God.

I knew what my barrier was...not trusting God enough to provide the support my children and I needed if I said yes and became a minister. I wrote the paragraph and turned in the paper. In the next session of the class we were instructed to go to see if we could resolve our dilemma.

The grounds contained a farm, a lake, and a large wooded area.

I chose to walk along a wooded path. It was outlined by pine trees that whistled when the wind blew and ancient oaks whose limbs danced instead of whistled.

I leaned against one of the oaks and said aloud, "God, I know you have urged me to be a minister, but I'm afraid. I don't know where the money will come from because the way I believe now no traditional church will hire me. I'd have to start my own church, and as you know, I can't afford that."

I sat and listened in silence. No response from God. This was a one-sided conversation.

I spoke again and said, "God, I really do want to please you. I would be honored to be a spokesperson for you. But I'm in need of some objective guidance, not my family, not my friends, not my professors. Can *you* help me?"

I felt someone watching me. Chills went up my spine. Being as quiet and still as possible, I cut my eyes to the left to see if someone was there. Nothing but trees.

I waited a minute and turned my eyes to the right. About twenty feet away was a large, antlered deer with huge brown eyes and eyelashes a model would die for.

The deer and I looked at each other. I didn't know if he was dangerous. I wanted to keep my distance so I could run back to the classroom if necessary.

I looked at the deer and said in a moderately loud voice, "Boo!"
The deer did not move.

I looked again and asked, "Are you by any chance here for me?"
The deer did not speak, move or respond in any way. He was so still I wondered if I had mistaken it for a statue.

"Ok, deer," I said, "do you have anything to say to me?"

Again, only stillness.

We both remained still, but our eye contact held firm. I took a deep breath and went for it.   "Mr. Deer, or whoever or whatever you are, am I to say *yes* to God, trust Him to support me, and be willing to become a pastor right now?"

Expecting nothing, the deer nodded his head up and down, up and down, over and over again in full and certain assent to my question.

When he quit nodding, he looked at me even more intensely like he was waiting for something.

I spoke again, "Ok, God, in front of this witness, you've got me for better or worse. I will go wherever you send me and do whatever you ask me to do. I commit myself to you completely."

The deer nodded once and ran into the woods. I felt a freedom, a lightness. A burden was lifted. A joy of anticipation took over my senses as I slid to the ground.

With tears rolling down my face I thought, *Good Lord, what have I done?*

When I regained my composure, I asked God, "Hey, is there any negotiating here?"

No answer from God, and the deer was gone.

I spoke again, "Lord, there is a caveat. I really do want to please you, but in your infinite wisdom if you could just agree to two stipulations I will leave today and do what is necessary to become an ordained minister."

No word from God or the deer.

Building courage, I prayed this prayer, "Lord, God, could I ask just these two favors? Please don't have me minister in Gulfport, Mississippi, and don't ever ask me to pass a collection plate, preach a stewardship sermon, or ask for money for whatever church I end up in?"

I took a deep breath and continued, "If I get up every day and do whatever you ask me to do, can I count on you to send the money needed without my asking for it? Amen."

The answer seemed so loud I was sure it had actually been spoken.

"Go home to Gulfport and your church is under your feet."

Under my feet?

"God, you want me to use my shed as a church? Where will I go?"

Again, a loud answer.

"There's a garage just around the corner from you. It'll do just fine."

The shed (above); my first duties as a minister (below)

34

Once again, Gail and I became sheet rockers. We transformed the garage by putting in two windows, carpeting the uneven concrete floor, painting the walls a bright white, and planting flowers along a handmade sidewalk.

I had a new home.

In converting my shed into a chapel, I removed my bed, couch, and TV and replaced those items with folding chairs. Gail and I found a coffee table, sans legs, and a rusted bottom of an old pedal sewing machine at a dump in New Orleans. We placed them together to make our altar.

Those two discarded remnants became a symbol for our ministry. Restoration and resurrection are always possible.

We were still decorating and remodeling the morning before my ordination. My sons, Neil and Jamie, drove down from Oxford to attend the ceremony and tour the new, one-room chapel. As I gave them a tour and explained to them both how Gail and I found and built the altar from scraps, they noticed that a huge portrait of their brother Harry still hung on the wall behind the altar.

Neil pointed to the painting and said, "Jamie, look, Mom has her own crucifixion scene with the savior!"

"Let's all worship Harry!" Jamie chimed in.

"Yes," Neil said in a whisper, "I hear he's never sinned."

As Jamie and Neil bent over in laughter, I removed the painting and hung a suitable wall decoration.

A portrait of Harry by Miriam Weems.
The painting remained over our altar prior to the opening of The Nourishing Place.

I was ordained on February 8, 1997. We held our first worship service that morning. At 9:00 a.m. when worship started, there were nine of us in attendance. As we began our worship, the bright February sun shone in through one of the shed's windows over the altar.

I glanced down at the floor and saw the words "New Home" mysteriously imprinted on the carpeted floor. I gazed in wonder and awe. The others saw it too. Someone pointed out it was the sun shining through the treadle of the New Home sewing machine base we were using as an altar.

It was holy confirmation. We were on the right path.

FIVE

35

Never having been much of a trusting person, it became clear to me there is no other way to live than to trust a God who knows you and your foibles and can use you in any way. That is freedom. But I am human.

The times in years past in which I have stubbornly refused to trust God, I got tangled in big messes. I feared finding another husband with weaknesses such as irresponsibility or an overwhelming desire to change me from a part-time thinker-doer to a full-time stay-at-home domestic with no pay and no benefits. I realized I did have a lot of love to give. I just wasn't discerning enough to choose one who loved me for me, warts and all.

One morning I was in my hot-tub on the patio. I prayed this simple prayer.

"God, if you do want me to have someone to share my life, then you have to select him."

The next day at lunch with my friend Max Peck, I asked, "Why have you never invited me out on a date?"

"I didn't think you would want to go out with me."

"Try me," I said.

He did.

• • •

By word of mouth, neighbors in our poverty level community came to The Nourishing Place to be nourished. A musical friend, Bill Kelly, made CDs for us. Each Sunday, the sounds of old hymns permeated our sacred space.

One Sunday he brought Gigi Hines to church. She, a black songbird, played the guitar and sang in nightclubs. And she began to sing for our church services.

Jo Kennedy cooked eggs, biscuits, grits, sausages, cakes and cookies. Before long, folks asked to take the leftovers home to have food for their evening meal. Soon we had to enclose the porch to make more sanctuary room. The breakfast moved into Gail's house. My friend Austin Lindsay came to assist Jo in cooking. More and more food found its way into the community. When we discovered clothing was needed, I asked people in the community to drop off things they no longer needed. We had a stocked give-away ministry. More people came and brought others who wanted to feel accepted in a church setting.

I recall that Floy once told me people always come home to the place that nourishes them. In spite of my love for the Gulf, the beach, the oak trees, the full moons, and colorful sunrises and sunsets, I did not want to come home to Gulfport. There was too much family history of goodness and respect to encounter. I did not feel I could live up to the ghosts of living spirits who had shaped me to be something I wasn't.

God got His way about where I was to be sent, and I got my way about not having to preach about money. I don't. I won't.

I have never passed a collection plate, preached a stewardship sermon, or asked for money. A ceramic dove, which once served as a small flowerpot on my sister Harriet's porch, sits on our altar. Each Sunday the dove is filled to overflowing with checks, cash and coins. Checks also come through the mail. Together, there is always enough and then some to do what God expects us to accomplish in the old, run down area of our ministry.

But I did come home to Gulfport.

• • •

Max took me to New York to meet his mother. During the two hour drive from Syracuse to Sidney, Max told me all of his vices. He claimed

Max Peck at his family plot in New York

to be lazy, of bad moods, loud, and obnoxious. He added that he drank too much, talked too much, and loved too little.

Then he said, "But if you want to get married I am willing."

I said nothing for a moment, then I burst out laughing.

"That is absolutely the worst proposal I've ever had!"

Max sulked.

"If you are willing go to the end of Courthouse Road pier, on a full moon night, get on your knees in front of a witness, and propose properly, I will say "yes."

Max and I married in the living room of the farmhouse where Captain Bob and Carmen Engram lived. Jo Kennedy was our only attendee… she brought the supper! On the way to the farm I asked Bob if he would give me away.

"Hell no!" he said, "I'll sell you for $24.95 cents."

In the car, we signed our marriage agreement. Bob signed it with Judge Eugene Henry as the witness and the officiator.

• • •

Of all the images I have of the entity I call God, the circle seems the most appropriate. A circle of love where everyone wins.

Max and I wanted to develop a primitive camp to teach children how to ride horses and appreciate nature.

One morning we set off for our usual morning horse ride through the Clower-Thornton Nature Trail that connected to my property. We usually stayed within the boundaries of the nature trail. This day, however, Max wanted to cross over 28th Street to explore a wooded area where we'd never been before.

As soon as Traveler and I set foot on that wooded stretch of land, we both shivered. Traveler stopped, looked around as did I. I knew we had entered holy land.

We rode all through the woods on small trails made by walkers not

Bob Engram, Jo Kennedy, Max and me at our wedding

horses. We stepped over fallen trees, jumped over creeks, and moved gently through brambles and scratchy bushes.

I knew this property would make a perfect primitive camp. I also knew, from exploring other land parcels in that neighborhood, that the lots were only 25 feet wide and 60 feet deep. I assumed I would have to look up hundreds of owners to see if any were willing to sell.

Monday morning came and I was at the door of the County Court-house before it opened. I walked straight to the tax assessor's office.

The secretary helped me find the owners. We discovered Hands-boro Presbyterian Church owned it all — three city blocks of woods! I couldn't believe it. One of my oldest friends, Stevie Wilson, was an elder in that church, so I called and asked him about the property.

He verified his church owned it all because he had spent years buy-ing up pieces of it and had given it all to the church. He asked me why I was interested.

"Our church," I explained, "wants to create a nature space and primitive camp for the at-risk children we serve. None of them have ever seen a raccoon, a cricket or a frog. And none have ever ridden a horse. We want to build a few cabins and tent sites and spend weekends there with the children."

"I wish I had known that," Stevie said," I would have given the property to your church instead of mine. But now, our church needs the funds to do some refurbishment of our facilities."

"How much are you asking?"

"We hope to get $78,000 for it," he said.

I thanked him and said that was way out of our price range, but that I enjoyed reconnecting with him.

Max and I spent the rest of that day trying to figure how to pur-chase the land, knowing our church did not have the funds, nor did I at that time.

We prayed about it for several weeks then an interesting bit of news came my way.

My tenant in Floy's house — the house I rented for income after my retirement was lost in the collapse of Coast Magazine Corporation — was Rev. John Shearer. He had ordained me.

Rev. Shearer was now the minister at Handsboro Presbyterian Church.

It occurred to me that maybe I could take the rent money Rev. Shearer gave me and give it to the Handsboro Presbyterian Church . . . which was paying the salary of Rev. Shearer.

From my hands to a church to a minster back into my hands.

All parties agreed. And we purchased the primitive camp.

That's what I call a circle of love.

However, by spending my rent income on the property meant I now had no income at all. Once again, a gift appeared in the form of Maxwell Corbin Peck, Jr. who had just married me.

"I want to set you free, Janie," he said, "to do what you feel called to do."

Max offered to support me! Oh My God! Support me?! As in pay my bills? Relieve my stress? Help me be *me*?

Max said he wanted to be the wind beneath my wings…and at that point Max started calling me *bird*. As in Hummingbird. Because I am never still.

36

I stand at the pulpit in front of eighty or so eclectic believers. I am their minister. The couple at the back are hallelujah, hand-raising Christians. They sway to the music with eyes closed and I can hear their mental drumbeat of "Jesus, Jesus, Jes*us*." I used to do that.

Across the aisle from them is a science fiction reader who thinks like Zechariah Sitchen that we were seeded here by aliens who have evolved into our God. They monitor our societal progress for an unknown reason. They may return someday to interact. We may be their meat, their slaves or their puppies. Max believes this too.

Our black participants sit in different places each Sunday. They came at first with hesitation, then exuberantly. Their churches encouraged shouting "Amen!" throughout the worship service. At my request, they now "Amen" in silence. Their shouts frightened the older Anglo-Saxon protestants; each shout caused a white-haired jumping bean reaction. I can still hear the "Amens" of my black brothers and sisters, because they nod their heads after each pleasing statement. I, too, used to say "Amen" during services at the churches I visited, but always under my breath, and only after I had attended a few charismatic Yoke Fellow workshops led by a man who truly believed in miracles, but never had money. He put the "touch" on us as we left each session.

Many in my congregation are old. Very old. We have partially blind and nearly deaf who sit scattered across the rows with their palms open like children hoping for candy. They want from me assurance. They want certainty, not just hope. I offer it to them with as much sincerity and integrity as I can muster. I understand. I used to want that, too.

A young newcomer is astounded by the Christian knick-knacks that cover our walls. Garish, colorful, handmade artifacts and antique items abound. Some are of no value. Others are priceless. Each one is a gift. Each one has great meaning.

Used-to-be-Catholics also come. They relish the idea of religious freedom and smile through each service, but I see them eyeing the peculiar sewing machine altar. It is absent of bread and wine. They leave feeling the service is not quite over.

Homeless men and women bravely come to the front of the chapel in filthy t-shirts which were new days ago, gifts from the largess of fellow worshipers. They sit comfortably next to older, clean women and well-to-do men.

I see the homeless man on the front row is restless. He smells the enticing aroma coming from the kitchen. Where most churches keep their sacred relics, the gold or silver plates and chalices for bread and wine, we cook. Behind our altar French toast bubbles in melted butter. In a few minutes, syrup will be poured generously by members of the congregation who have serving hearts. This is our Eucharist. Jesus himself must surely delight in this barrier-breaking communion. Black, white, Latino, young and old, rich and poor, homeless and well-housed sit side by side, sharing butter-drenched food, touching one another with affection and laughter. In addition to the French toast the scrambled eggs, sausages, biscuits and gravy, sliced bananas and tropical fruits, juice and coffee, our typical Sunday spread, are the wine and bread of the Eucharist. It is a feast of Thanksgiving in the most basic of ways. It is in these few moments each Sunday, when plates filled high with goodies from the earth's bounty nourish bodies, and unconditional acceptance of each other nourishes souls and creates unity. This weekly fellowship of doubters and believers is a nearly perfect parable of the alive, vibrant body of the risen Christ.

As an ordained minister in a Christian church, being multi-divorced, multi-married, is a difficult state of affairs. I understand a minister of God's church is expected to be a "nice" lady, meaning unsullied and monogamous. Since I'm neither, I've found the best guard against possible slights from my congregation is to be on the offensive.

When I first set foot in the pulpit I started my initial sermon with these words:

"God is not religious. Jesus was never a Christian. The Bible is a library containing stories of fiction, legends, myth and symbols all indicating truth, but not factual in and of themselves. And, by the way, your new minister is the worst sinner in the church."

No one has yet left because of my resemblance to Madame Bovary. On the contrary, my congregates seem to take great hope in the fact that God allows me to teach about Him. Obviously my sins have been forgiven. So if I can be forgiven, maybe they can too.

The opportunity to share and lead worship with this loving, supportive, gregarious group thrills me. I am passionate about them in a way I never thought possible. I've seen their fears. I've heard their beliefs. I've been by their side in joy and grief. I know what many of them think and what most of them hope for. My desire is to open a window in their minds, clear out the false teachings they harbor, and set them free. I want to lead them to enlightenment. Their own enlightenment. I try to do this in bits and pieces. Sometimes it sends them running away from my words. I speak of the humanity of Jesus, the fact that often, day and night, his mom had to change his swaddling clothes when he was an infant. A few traditionalists did not want to hear that. Surely, Jesus was above bodily functions. Later, I offered the possibility that Jesus fell in love like we all do, maybe more than once. Some don't yet accept the normality of Jesus. So I back off for a while and talk about His holiness and our own, yet in words that are more acceptable, less uncomfortable. Sometimes their un-readiness frustrates me, as my own once did. I sense their faith is not yet strong enough. I protect them from themselves, for now. But one day I will stop. One day I will bar the back the door and tell them. I'm going to tell them the truth, the whole truth and nothing but the truth.

Daily I search scripture for messages of hope and love, forgiveness and peace. I read books by Spong, Borg, Whitehead, Ian Thomas, Rohr, and others who set Jesus free from his 2000-year image of being divine from birth. Their spiritual insights offer Jesus to others as a powerful spiritual God resurrected in us, his disciples. These biblical scholars encourage believers to set Christ free from the limitations placed on him by the agendas, space and time he humanly inhabited. My desire is to blow out the cobwebs of an exclusive theology in order to birth a loving spirit in each of us that is non-dogmatic, non-doctrinal, non-creedal, hopeful and ever expanding to be inclusive in every way.

Every person who enters the church is hugged. By many, not just me. It is vital that gatherers, whether they are true believers or not, are treated with respect, hugs, and dignity. Sometimes it's difficult, especially when Lola comes hung over and falls out of her chair into a heap on the floor, or bearded Martha Ann puts three plates of food in her purse prior to worship. However, our mission is to forgive and love all people, all acts, all the time. Our goal is unconditional love.

Without a doubt, I could search the world over and not find a group more loving, more accepting, more tolerant, more compassionate or more hopeful than "my people." I am blessed to know and serve them.

My son Harry thinks our congregational life improves the spiritual equilibrium of Mississippi, where country clubs have mattered for too long.

Like most ministers, I am gratified when I am affirmed for my beliefs and my teachings. For example, one Tuesday night during Bible Study, the lesson was on the transfiguration of Jesus. I explained that when each of us realizes we have the power to change our behavior through the guidance of the Holy Spirit within, we become purer, more ethical, more like Jesus.

In the midst of my explanation, Linda, a 50 year old ex-marine, jumped up from the fourth row and raised her arms in the air.

"I get it!" she shouted. "Ever since I started coming here to church, I have changed. I am not half the slut I used to be."

Well . . . truth be told, neither am I.

37

Many times I have no idea how to present comfort and/or assistance in the manner in which a person will accept. Most of the work I do outside of preaching and teaching Bible Study is to listen to people and offer guidance, if possible, or suggest a certified counselor if I think that is more useful. Most people who call for an appointment want to have some pre-marital discussions or to be consoled through bereavement. I handle these discussions adequately. At least, I feel prepared for these types of discussions.

A woman called and asked for a meeting with me. She had a problem and wanted religious counseling.

I made it clear that I was not a certified counselor, rather a teaching minister, but I would be glad to listen and perhaps recommend a professional counselor. She said she didn't want to go to a counselor, because she wanted religious answers not psychological ones. We set up the meeting for 10:00 o'clock the next morning at the Nourishing Place's chapel.

When the lady came in the door, I noticed she was not particularly attractive. She dressed stylishly but prudishly. Her blouse was buttoned all the way to the top, her arms were completely covered with a tight cuff at her wrist. She had on sheer stockings and high heels. Her smile was bright and full, showing straight white teeth. Her dark brown hair was lustrous and pulled back into a smooth pony tail. We sat down, I poured coffee for us, then asked her to tell me about herself.

She began her story. "My husband died ten years ago and I am lonely. I haven't had a date in all those years. I have a few friends from work but they are all women and all are married. My nights and weekends are boring, dull. I need more in my life."

I thought this sounded normal, and I hoped I could assist her in some way. "I know how painful loneliness can be. Sometimes it seems to stifle you. In fact, loneliness can make you feel more isolated than you truly are. But, tell me, what do you do to entertain yourself?" I asked with compassion in my voice.

"Well," she said in a quiet voice, "that's why I'm here. I just want to make sure that what I am doing is okay with God. You know I'm not really religious but I don't want to go to hell."

I thought perhaps she was going to tell me she was involved with a married man. I was prepared to hear that because I hear it often in my line of work. It also triggered a desire to tell her I did not believe in a typical hell, one that most people seem to need. I judiciously thought that conversation could wait. I took her by the hands and said, "Just tell me what your struggle is and let's talk through it."

She pulled her hands away, placed them in her lap, and held them together so tightly her knuckles were white and purplish. "OK," she said. "Lately I have been involved in oral sex."

I nodded my head for her to continue.

"With my dog," she said.

I paused for a second and then did a ministerial no-no. I burst out laughing, guffawing! I could not stop. I shook with laughter. Tears ran down my face. The prurient side of me wanted details: what kind of dog is he? Is he a handsome dog? How old is he? Where does this liaison take place? Oh, God I had to get control of myself, but thank heavens by now she was laughing with me.

We finally hiccupped to a stop and I said in my most apologetic voice, "I regret I laughed at your dilemma. Please forgive me. But even worse, I haven't a clue of what to say to you. You've thrown a bomb at my practiced religious responses."

She pushed the hair off her shoulder. "It's kind of sick, isn't it? Then she asked, "Am I going to hell?"

Catching my breath and trying not to be too academic, I said, "Let's look at this in two ways. First, biblically speaking, as far back as Abraham and Lot, maybe 3500 years ago, sodomy was considered a sin. In fact, God destroyed Sodom and Gomorrah because of illegal sexual practices. Having a sexual encounter with a non-human is called bestiality, and it too was and maybe is still a sin. As far as that goes, you either take the biblical definition of sodomy as sin, repent and ask for forgiveness of God and yourself and don't do it again. Or you talk to God about your situation and see if there is a healthier, more self-loving way for you to be … errrrr … entertained. Also, keep in mind those sexual laws were man-made to ensure their tribe would survive. They needed to grow their own labor force and their own army. Therefore, sexual activities such as masturbation, homosexuality and bestiality were forbidden because they prevented needed human reproduction.

Without any hesitation, she asked, "What's the second way to look at it?"

I continued my spiel. "A second consideration is that hell is a complex idea with many varying explanations and definitions. I think hell is perhaps more man made than God made. At least that is my current way of thinking. I believe God does not punish us at all, ever, for any sin. Rather the sin we commit punishes us. You see, because you have chosen this way to relieve your sexual desires, and it seems to satisfy you, you have barred yourself from seeking healthier, happier ways to have your needs met."

"So there is no hell?" she asked.

"Let me put it this way. Hell traditionally means some kind of punishment or revenge for a person who has done something illegal, immoral, unethical, or sinful. We do have consequences for our wrong, hurtful choices. However, I think it is usually the choices themselves that punish us. That is the hell we create for ourselves.

With a sharpness in her tone she asked, "What kind of pastor are you? I've never heard any of these explanations before."

My answer was, "I try to be a loving, comforting, encouraging person. Many times I fail." She thanked me for my time, said she would consider my recommendations. I walked her to her car and bid her a God-Bless-You good-bye. I did not hear from her again. I prayed she would find what she needed.

Walking back into the chapel I chastised my self. I can't believe I laughed at her in her misery. I knelt at the altar and asked God to forgive my pitiful efforts and to have mercy on me. Maybe I needed to find a less challenging job.

I sat in the kitchen for a while, brewed a cup of coffee, and jotted down some ideas. The first thought was to acknowledge there is a vast difference between Religion and Spirituality, between man-made dogma and God's unlimited love and forgiveness. I wanted to explore these ideas with my congregation and together live into Spirituality rather than Religion. Spirituality seemed more holy yet more humane than Religion. The second idea was if I wanted to be a competent minister I needed to be more courageous, to speak openly about my desire to bring Jesus out of the clouds, out of a preordained, pre-existent divinity. I wanted to show him as a wholly, 100%, human in every way, just like the rest of us billion humans. My desire was to convey the concept that only an authentic, honest, real-life Jesus, who chose a path of unconditional love at the cost of his life, could ever truly help, guide, and save us from ourselves.

38

After six years in the shed and porch and other added on rooms, we moved. Max, who at that time had retired from the FAA and worked in the courthouse as a bailiff, heard about some property which had on it a dilapidated church surrounded by massive live oak trees. It was being sold for taxes. It was only four blocks from our current church. Max got the name and number of the woman who owned the property. Trying to do a kind deed, I telephoned the woman who owned the property to ask if she knew it was being sold for taxes in just three weeks.

"Shit. You are a damn busy-body." She hung up on me.

Later, I forgave her and called again. This time she listened to me. She hollered into the phone.

"If you want it so bad pay me 50 grand and you can have the shit hole."

I gave her my phone number in case she decided to sell it for less. She hung up on me again.

That night, her husband called to say they would sell the property for $7,000.00. I thanked him but said, "We don't have funds in that amount."

One day later, Max's income tax refund came in. The check was in the amount of $7,700.00. We purchased the property and waited.

The congregation asked, "How will we rebuild the church without money?"

My response was, "If it is to be a place of worship, God will provide the money."

My friend, Tom Brosig, and his wife, Judge Robin Midcalf, invited me to lunch. They too, asked what we were going to do with the old church building.

I replied, "God will provide the way."

Tom operated a casino which many people in this Baptist Bible Belt thought was a sinful enterprise. Tom said, "God has provided the way. The way is my casino. If you and Max borrow the money for the materials, my staff and I will build your church." And they did. Bob Kelly, a vice president of all the Grand Casinos in America, bought the lighting fixtures. He did the electrical work himself. Tom and his staff built the interior and bricked the outside. Before the $40,000.00 note Max and I borrowed came due, Drew Allen, who is president of Allen Beverages and who attended The Nourishing Place, informed me the Pepsi Cola Company had given his plant money to spend in the community. He paid off the loan. Max and I put the property in the name of the not-for-profit, charitable agency, The Nourishing Place.

Our location is four blocks north of the white, sandy beaches of the Gulf of Mexico. Purple streaked, golden sunrises brighten potholed streets. Our street is lined by majestic, moss-draped oak trees, hundreds of years old, and is gated by a vacant, debris strewn lot on the corner and a dilapidated blue 7-11 store that is robbed more often than not.

This old area of Gulfport is sacred ground to me. It was here that my great-grandfather Tushoyan's ancestors, native Choctaw Indians, lived in their deerskin and palmetto leaf shelters. They were here at the water's edge with their flattened Choctaw heads, high cheek bones, and skimpy coon-skin loin cloths, watching D'Iberville and Beinville's frigates come ashore, changing their world for all time. It was here on these sand beaches that Floy, Tushoyan's daughter, taught me life lessons, that if I had lived them I would not have left a trail of creation and destruction behind me, harming those I loved most.

The Nourishing Place

• • •

My sister Harriet had suffered from breast cancer for years, but it was in remission until 2001. That's when she had a double mastectomy.

But she maintained high spirits. Harriet did not want anyone "fussing" over her or making her feel like an invalid. After her husband Leland died, Harriet spent more time with Max and me. Max adored Harriet, and the feeling was mutual.

One afternoon, Harriet had a fainting spell, almost like a seizure. I was concerned and asked if I could take her to Keesler Air Base hospital to her doctor. Surprisingly, she agreed.

As we drove down the beach to Keesler Harriet was unusually quiet.

"Are you ok?" I asked.

"Not really," she said. "Lately I've been dizzy and I think at times I hallucinate. I see things like birds in the house that I know are not really there."

"Well, Harriet, you have to tell your doctor about that."

When we arrived at Keesler, we waited for her doctor. She went in and I waited for at least two hours.

Harriet didn't like coming to my church. She thought it was dangerous for me to "interpret" the bible. She was confortable with her literal beliefs. She knew a golden highway waited for her in the sky. She worried about me, I know.

But I wasn't the only one Harriet worried about. She told Neil III that she was worried about his son, Neil IV, going off to college in Princeton, New Jersey.

"Why?" Neil III asked her.

"I'm afraid he's going to go up there and become a liberal," she said.

Soon a nurse came out and told me they were going to admit Harriet for observation and some tests. They asked if could I bring Harriet some night clothes and toiletries.

I went to her house, gathered the things she might need and took them back to her. She was sitting up in bed.

"Listen, Jane. I'm not afraid of dying, but I am afraid of the process of getting sicker and sicker."

"I know you must be, but don't jump to conclusions. Let's wait and see what these new tests tell us."

I stayed with her until suppertime then went home. Max and I prayed for Harriet during our blessing.

The next morning I went back to the hospital. When I went in the room her doctor and two nurses were with her. The doctor motioned for me to follow him out to the hall.

"Your sister is a sick lady," he said. "The cancer has spread and it is in her brain and spinal cord. We will send her home but she must have a caretaker. Each day it will be harder for her to care for herself."

I felt sick. Dismayed.

"Thank you, Doctor," I said. "I will take her home to live with me. We will see that she has everything she needs."

Several days later, Harriet was discharged from the hospital and I took her to our house.

On the way, we stopped at her home to get a few more things she might need. Before we arrived back at my house Harriet said, "I'll just be here a day or two until I get stronger. I don't want to be a burden to you or Max. So just plan on taking me home this weekend."

"You silly thing. You will never be a burden to either of us. We want you with us full time. It will be fun to be together."

And for a while it was.

The doctor was right. Each day Harriet became weaker and more confused. I called my four children to tell them about the diagnosis and that they probably needed to come see Harriet as soon as they could.

They got together and sent Neil III photos of themselves with Harriet. Each child wrote a note to her about how good Harriet had been to them, how they had benefitted from her gifts of money and trips and loving support. Neil put all their comments and photos in a book. A couple of weeks later Neil, Liz, Jamie and families arrived. Harry was on tour in Europe and could not make it home at that time, but he called to talk to Harriet.

We had a party with Harriet as the honoree and each person read their comments to her. She told them to stop being maudlin. The next week we hired a nurse to come stay with Harriet from noon to midnight. I could handle the morning hours and when she was asleep. Harriet required more and more morphine. Her friends came and sat with her. Read to her and shared fond memories. I'm not sure Harriet even heard them.

One night, Neil and his wife Debbie, Jamie, and Liz were all home. Each one went to Harriet's bedside to tell her goodnight. It was their goodbye to her. When the last ones left at 11:00, I headed to the back bedroom. I walked right past Harriet's door. Then I stopped. I backed up and went in her room. She was sleeping and the nurse was sitting next to her holding her hand. I walked over to Harriet's side of the bed and took her other hand. I held it as she took her last breath.

We held her funeral at The Nourishing Place on her birthday March 5, 2005.

I missed her. My last close family relative was gone. I was now the oldest person, the matriarch of my clan. The Stanley name had daughtered out.

I thought of Harriet almost constantly for the next month. I marveled at her steadfastness. She was, like my daddy, the most ethical person I knew. She was a physical education teacher before she retired, so she never earned much money. But she was the one who paid for my children's camp and travel experiences, their instruments and music lessons, helped with their college tuition, and paid Liz's $2000 of parking tickets from Ole Miss.

My four grown children (L to R) Jamie, Neil, Liz, and Harry

She had doted on Katie, Liz's daughter, and called Katie her baby. Katie never lacked for anything. In fact, in her will, Harriet left all my children thousands of dollars each.

She was truly their angel and in many ways their earthly savior.

39

Sunday, August 28, Gulf Coast residents were fleeing the approaching storm. Thousands of cars jammed Highway 49, I-10, I-59 attempting to arrive somewhere north of the coast to ride out the storm. Having gone through many hurricanes before, I chose to stay in our home. Max agreed. We busied ourselves with stacking fresh bottles of water, purchasing new flashlights and batteries, making sure we had enough peanut butter, jelly and bread in our cabinets, and moving books away from the bottom shelves of our glassed in den just in case the creek behind our house rose out of its bounds. That had never happened before. Max loaded the horses and took them to Big Fred's farm north of Carriere, MS.

Late Sunday afternoon we began to feel the first winds of the storm. The media was constantly warning us to get to safety! Batten down the hatches! Board up windows while you can! The storm is huge, covering most of the Gulf and winds were up to 125 mph with gusts much higher. We began to get family members and friends out of their homes and into ours. My son Jamie in the National Guard, preparing to be deployed to Kuwait, was in Hattiesburg at Camp Shelby.

He insisted his wife Heather, their 4 year old daughter Camille and 10 day old Charlie move into our house, which was farther away from the beach than theirs.

My step-mother Rachel Stanley and her friend Agnes brought pillows and blankets and moved in. Neighbors Joan and Stephen Lindh came with flashlights and little else. About 3:30 p.m. Robin Denny called and pleaded with us to get her parents Bob and Carmen Engram to leave their home (right off the beach) and bring them home with us. The Engrams did not want to leave. However, after the third daughter called and literally begged them to leave, they reluctantly allowed Max to come pick them up. They moved in. We put a mattress on the floor of the living room for Bob and Carmen. Rachel and Agnes selected the two living room recliners as their beds. Joan took the couch in the den and Stephen chose a large lounge chair. We gave the guest bedroom to Heather and the children. Gail put a cot in the den to watch the trees in the woods bend and break. Max and I stayed in our back bedroom. We shared a supper of sandwiches, talked about previous hurricanes, and decided an early night might prove beneficial. With flashlights close by, we all tried to sleep.

That was impossible. The winds howled, trees fell, electricity shut off. Utter darkness. We huddled around Carmen's battery operated black and white tv. Disaster everywhere. Pictures of water surging over the beach highways. Then a huge crash as we watched the roof of the tv station collapse. No more television. More trees fell. One on top of my car. With no fans or air conditioners the heat oppressed us. At dawn we looked down our street and it was impassable with trees, limbs, debris.

Our fences where we kept the horses were down and the water continued to rise. Camille stood at the glassed-in door of the den and watched a turtle swim, banging its head on the door. The water was three feet high by then. She wanted to open the door to let the turtle in...but we all jumped to stop her. We hoped the door would hold the water at bay. It did not. Jamie's beloved Retriever Josie was on the porch of our storage unit and water was up to his neck. Stephen went out our front door, walked around back and carried Josie to the garage and put him in the back of Max's huge Ram truck for safety.

As the water slowly began to recede, Don Pizzetta, who lived on the beach, walked through debris and mud to tell us the bad news. His lovely antebellum home on the beach had been totally destroyed. He asked Max to tell the Engrams their house no longer existed.

Max asked the Engrams to come to the den as we all stood around to lend support.

Don said, "I hate to tell you this but your house is gone, washed away. And looters are already picking up loose items."

Carmen said, "What do you mean our house is gone? What about our cars? Our furniture?"

Don shook his head, "Miss Carmen, there is nothing left on your lot."

No tears were shed by either Engram.

Instead, Bob took Carmen's hands in his and said, "Don't worry, Sweetheart, we still have each other."

The rest of us wept like babies.

Max, the Engrams, and Stephen left the house and walked to the beach. It took hours to climb over trees, limbs, roof debris. What they discovered were houses on the railroad track, cars turned upside down blocks from where they belonged, and not a single beach house was left standing.

We heard later that Don had left, swam across Brickyard Bayou to get to his wife who was staying with her mother in Bayou View.

We were all stunned. Shaken. Hot. Sweaty. Even our clothes were damp. The stillness after the storm was deafening.

Our next order of business was to get each person to go out to the woods on the side of our house and pick their own toilet spot. Thank God we had sufficient downed logs to sit on separated from one another. Max made an outdoor kitchen on our large deck between the house and garage.

Heather and I drove to the National Guard AVCRAD Center, by dodging debris and closed roads, to find out if and when she could contact Jamie. She was desperate. She wanted to get to Alabama to stay with her Aunt Shirley who had electricity, air conditioning, and a safe place for her kids. The guard at the AVCRAD gate could not help us. Stephen, Heather, Camille and I, holding Charlie, drove the back roads toward Southern Circle where Jamie and Heather lived. We parked two blocks away and climbed over the railroad tracks to their home. The first thing we saw was a huge oak tree on the roof of the house and second we noticed an enormous arched roof support of the Country Club's club house on the street in front of the home.

We went in the back door. Camille rushed to her room where the oak tree had landed.

She screamed, "Mama, my room is broken!"

When we got back to our house, Heather was sitting on the back steps praying she would hear from Jamie. She needed to know he was OK and to tell him she would leave for Alabama as soon as possible.

Max with a chain saw and I with clippers were trying to dislodge my car. I looked up and saw a dessert sand colored army jeep come flying around the corner.

Before it even stopped Jamie was out of the driver's seat calling "Heather, Heather, where are you??" She heard him, jumped and ran so fast she careened into him sending them both to the ground. Camille right behind her flew into her daddy's arms. I left to pick up Charlie so he could be in the family embrace.

Within an hour, Jamie had loaded his family into their car and drove north to reach east Alabama.

There was no phone service. I could not reach Neil in Oxford, Liz in Meridian, Harry in Switzerland or son Max in Amarillo. I knew they were all trying to reach us and I could not fix the problem.

Evidently, Jamie had safely put his family in Alabama and somehow he had contacted Neil who picked up Jamie in Alabama. They found a trailer and rescued us. Seldom has there ever been a more welcomed sight than my two sons unloading water, gas, food, clean sheets, and a portable generator!

They helped rip the carpet off the den floor, made makeshift tables, and loaded them down with pasta, breads, peanut butter jars, jellies, Kool-aid, potatoes, charcoal for grills, and almost every other kind of survival foods.

When they unloaded they walked to the beach. Neil came back stunned beyond belief. Houses were topsy turvy everywhere. The house we had once lived in on Hewes Avenue was gone except for the upstairs porch, which rested across the railroad tracks. Neil came back and reported that the beach was covered with what looked like tiny arms sticking up for miles. The frozen chicken storage unit at the harbor two miles away had broken loose and dumped its contents up and down the beach. Neil said the stench was unbearable, as was the heat.

In many ways, I was glad Harriet wasn't alive to see the devastation Katrina caused. She was first and foremost a fixer. If something or someone was broken she could not sleep until she fixed, repaired, or corrected the problem. The un-fixable disarray, destruction, and chaos would have been her undoing.

I walked to our chapel four blocks away and discovered it was not damaged. It immediately became a distribution center. People brought food from freezers, dry towels, and canned goods by the hundreds. Other neighbors came to get what they needed and often brought other things in exchange.

On the third day, I woke up at 4 a.m. covered with an itchy, swelling rash. I knew I needed help. I drove to the chapel where Gail had spent the night and asked her to drive me to the hospital. A normally 15 minute drive took over an hour. We zigged zagged our way to Broad Avenue going the back roads. The beach roads were impassable. The hospital turned out to be a large white tent in the parking lot. A young doctor who had been sent down from Jackson looked at my rash, examined my hands and rubbed the palms of my hands over and over.

"Mrs. Stanley, I have very bad news for you," he said, shaking his head. "You seem to have syphilis!"

"What!? You have to be kidding. I do not have syphilis. Please, let me have a second opinion."

He left the room. Gail and I squealed with laughter. At least we hoped his diagnosis was a joke. It took nearly an hour, but finally an elderly doctor came in.

Looked me over and with a gentle smile said, "Not to worry. You don't have syphilis. However, rashes on the palms of hands are one symptom of syphilis." He asked me if I was allergic to any medicines. I said I was not.

"You have obviously come in contact with something you are allergic to. I don't know what it could be but I will give you some shots that might alleviate the itching and other symptoms." He gave me a tetanus, typhoid, steroid, two other shots, and sent me home. By the end of the day I had improved.

But there was no way to get dry!

The money started flowing into the church Post Office Box. Tom Brosig had contacted his friends in New York, the ones who sat on boards of corporations and industries. The first two checks from New York were $50,000 each. More came. Between the months of August and the end of December The Nourishing Place had received more than half a million dollars in donations. Many were sent to us because we have almost no overhead. We don't pay salaries or benefits and our facility is paid for. Therefore, the money that comes in goes directly out to the community. Our donors appreciate that their money is spent on real needs rather than administration. With the donations we purchased blue tarps to cover roofs on houses over a six block area.

Another friend of Tom's from Minnesota sent two 18-wheelers full of food, clothing, bedding, shoes, and household items. We opened the doors of the first one and invited people to come take what they needed.

We sent the other one to a church in Moss Point that had received no assistance. Then another 18-wheeler came. We took what was needed for our close-by neighborhoods and sent the rest to a Wiggins church whose members were in great need.

Donations flowed in from Japan, Austria, Switzerland, California, Tennessee, Arizona and north Mississippi. We took photographs of the houses, the blue tarps, the refrigerators and washing machines we purchased for families who were still trying to live at home. We sent these photos to donors so they could see first-hand the assistance they provided.

Emergency medical facilities in double-wide trailers cropped up on Pass Road…one every few blocks. I awoke one morning with a sore throat and fever. I went to the closest medical trailer. It was a little before 1 pm. The sign on the door informed us the facility was closed until 1:00. I waited. I heard voices inside the trailer. The nurse and doctor were speaking, the doctor in a rather loud voice. I heard him exclaim he needed a 55 gallon drum of Prozac because that's what every one on the coast seemed to need.

When the door opened and I saw the doctor, he greeted me, "Hello, what can I do for you." With a grin I said, "I need some Prozac."

He laughed and replied, "Oh, so you heard what I said.'

"Yes, and I agree with you. However, I came because I need something for fever and a sore throat." I left with a hand-full of assorted pills, grateful to have them.

Each evening our deck was the gathering spot. Ten or twelve people came and shared a meal…whatever we had, usually pasta and occasionally hamburgers and hot dogs if they had not been thawed out for too long. It was a time of fellowship, inquiring about families we had not heard from and wondering when lights and phone would be available. Judge Robin Midcalf came by. Her cell phone worked. She allowed me to call my son Harry in Switzerland.

When he came to the phone and heard my voice he screamed, "Oh,

Mama. Oh, I'm so thrilled to hear from you. Are you all right? Did you survive? Did the house survive?"

The questions went on and on with me attempting to say "Yes" after each one.

Then Harry said, "I wish I could be there to help."

Each week brought a new dilemma. Grocery stores opened slowly with little to offer. Water was being distributed in different locales every day. The parking lot in front of K-Mart still had a foot of water in it and people were bathing in the hot water, washing clothes in it, and some just lying in it hoping to cool down a bit.

It was two and a half weeks before electricity came on. Such jubilation! We drained the hot tub and put fresh water in it. Cleaned and cooled the house with the rejuvenated air conditioners. Our homeless friend David appeared having lost his few belongings and he moved in taking Heather and the children's place. Betty Bittner and Jo Kennedy arranged to pick up my step mother Rachel and her kitty cat and drive her to Mobile on the back roads to send her to California to stay with her daughter Mary Margaret.

Bob and Carmen Engram left for two weeks to stay in Dallas with Robin. When they returned they moved in with us for nearly 4 months. Our time together was a blessing. Most days after working and tending to the needs of the community we tired out about four in the afternoon. The four of us sat knee to knee in our 9x9 sunroom and discussed the day, laughed at the chaos that surrounded us, and grew close as a family should be.

Jamie was shipped off to Kuwait. Neil brought two more trailer loads of foods and aid and one more generator. Liz played hostess to her husband's family from New Orleans and 10 of them slept in her garage for 4 weeks. Thankfully she had a swimming pool that cooled them down after a day's labor. Max III from Texas had his youth group from his church come a few months later and help clear debris, stack limbs, and help paint our church's back porch that was the distribution center.

Finally, roads were cleared and the beach road repaved. Heather hired a contractor to replace their roof and repair Camille's broken room. Camille busied herself playing storm by lining her dolls up in the hallway then yelling at them to "duck, get out! The storm's coming."

Kept her busy for days.

Max had enrolled in nursing school at Mississippi Gulf Coast Community College. Week three they opened for school again but without electricity and without most toilets. Some of the young single mothers lived in their cars with their children. Our church bought them Wal-mart cards to purchase gas, groceries, books and other items needed while they literally camped out for weeks in the parking lot, using the car for beds and playpens.

Slowly, week by week, more amenities reopened. Driving became somewhat safer. Schools opened late but provided safe havens for the young ones. Our church continued and to this day still serves as a distribution center where clothing, canned goods, household items, linens and beddings, small appliances and furniture can be had free of cost for any who need that support.

The porch is open and stocked 24/7. A true blessing to the community.

40

In 2014, Max and I traveled to Zurich, Switzerland to see our son Harry and his partner Jens. One evening Jens prepared a gourmet meal of salad, homemade pasta and garden tomatoes. He had grown the vegetables in his garden.

The wine flowed as we enjoyed the crusted German bread and Danish butter. Jens' elderly parents, Ernst and Bethli, joined us for the evening. Even though we spoke no German and they spoke very little English, we managed to laugh together and consider the weariness of the world in which we all lived.

When dinner was over, as usual, I asked Harry to play a little saxophone music for us. He plays a Buescher saxophone from the 1920's, and uses the kind of mouthpiece Adolph Sax himself designed. Unlike most saxophonists, Harry plays classical and modern classical music. The sounds he produces on his saxophone are much like human voices, expressing the range of emotions our own voices convey.

He said he and Jens had prepared a piano-saxophone duet just for us. Jens sat at the piano and began playing the hauntingly beautiful Irish tune "Down by the Salley Gardens."

On the second verse, Bethli stood up, went to stand by Jens and began to sing the words, of course in German. She had a light, lilting soprano voice. In a few minutes, Ernst struggled out of his chair, shuffled over, took Bethli's hand in his, and began to sing the tenor part. The two of them looked at each other with such love it was tangible five feet away where

Max and I were sitting.

The four of them continued the sweetest concert I had ever heard. I looked at Max and tears were rolling down his face, matching mine tear for tear. I couldn't breathe.

When the music ended no one spoke. I think each of us realized we had shared a thin moment of musical grace and passionate love. During their six decades of marriage Ernst and Bethli had sung together often, in the Zurich Oratorio Choir, in church and on family trips to places like Denmark or the Bernese Alps.

That moment in Zurich reminded me, once again, we don't have to be in a church, temple, or mosque to experience sacred, holy moments.

We simply must be open to receiving them when they appear as unexpected gifts. Gifts from beyond our realm of existence, yet fully known through our humanity.

41

One night I was in an elusive, esoteric mood. While Max slept next to me, my mind ran rampant with trivial information. Yet, at the time, it seemed to be important to me.

I've been with Max for twenty years and I still think I ought to share everything.

I gently nudged Max awake. "What was Moses' last name?" I asked.

In a groggy voice, he all but shouted, "Moses, who?"

"Moses in the Bible."

"That Jewish guy?" he asked.

"Yeah, him," I replied.

"I don't know," he paused. "Berkowitz, I guess. Now go back to sleep!"

I thought how strange it was that of the thousands of characters in our Christian Bible, no one, not one single person had a last name. If they had been Europeans rather than desert folk they would have had last names depending on the work they did.

Saul/Paul's last name might have been "Leatherman."

Peter's last name could have been "Fisher."

Jesus would have had several possibilities for his last name. One might have been Carpenter. Another Stoneworker. Or maybe Walker. Yes, I liked that one the best. Some of my favorite friends had the last name of Walker. Jesus Walker sounded just right.

Then I turned to Mary and Joseph. I thought perhaps they would have been stuck with Carpenter or Stoneworker. Then maybe Jesus would have had to have a hyphenated name to be recognized by his broader family. Perhaps Jesus Carpenter-Walker would have been appropriate.

Then I thought of King David. He was a shepherd then a king, so his last name could have been Shepherd or King.

Wanting to share this with my sleeping husband, I again gently nudged Max.

"Which last name do you think David would have chosen: David King or David Shepherd.

"How the hell should I know? You're the preacher!"

• • •

Some mornings sitting in the swing in my lush patio cathedral, drenched in dawn's purple rays, I reminisce about thin moments and thin times when I connect with a primordial world. I remember my first aware-ness of such a world. I was a lithe, blossoming 15 year old.

It was a full moon night. A group of friends had gone to the beach to play "Spin the Bottle." I was too shy to play. Wandering off by myself I stood in the shallow water facing the Gulf's horizon. In the western sky, the pink sunset faded. As I turned east, an April full moon in all its brightness rose. The lunar light on the water was like diamonds shimmering a pathway from the moon to me. It seemed like no distance at all. A Gulf breeze ca-ressed me, heavy and warm. The ebb tide of salty water pulled the sand from under my feet so that my toes sunk deeper into the earthy, sandy wet-ness. Seagulls wheeled overhead. At that moment I knew I was in harmony with the world around me. I was not alone. I was one with breath and air, stars and shrimp boat lights, friends kissing on the beach. I felt greater than myself. In that mystical night air, I looked up in silence through the stars and felt imbued with a life greater than just my own.

In thin times, tears well up from deep within me.

Those tears connect my cosmic memory to an enlightening now. I tremble in awe as a lump in my throat or a catch in my breath let me know that I have inherent meaning and purpose.

During one of my morning reflections, my memory landed on spirit-filled quadrangles. Once again wanting to share a holy moment, I reverently whispered to husband Max. "Quadrangles always make me cry."

Silence. Then, Max moved aside the newspaper he was reading.

"What did you say?"

"Quadrangles always make me cry," I repeated.

"Yep, Janie-Bird," he said, "circles, squares, and pentagons tear me up, too."

We are not always on the same wavelength. In truth, we seldom are. Max is 200 plus pounds of intelligence and humor. He holds on to me like a kite to keep me from soaring away into the wooing world of visions and imagination. He thinks I prefer that realm to his stark reality.

He is right.

Max is a gift to me from the Ultimate Benign. After four failed marriages with three men, I was determined not to marry again.

Different as we are — I, a people pleaser; he, a people agitator — our relationship works. And we work at it.

I believe and adhere to non-literal, iconic biblical teachings and their ultimate, deep truth. Max is a lapsed Lutheran who believes humans were seeded by space aliens who gave innate, non-alterable toolboxes for dealing with life.

In his defense, the sixth chapter of Genesis does tell about the Nefilim giant who came to earth from the sky, had intercourse with earthly females, thus creating Homo Sapiens. Statues of these giants are currently being uncovered around the world.

Our disparate ideas create stimulating conversations over candlelight dinners of shrimp gumbo, fried and buttered cornbread and several glasses of Chardonnay, my preference — vodka, his.

I do not take spirituality lightly. True spirituality is firmly grounded in humanity, even in our own frail and fraudulent attempts at being humanely human. Spirit permeates us all; it is a cellular thing.

Pierre Teilhard deChardin, a priest, geologist, and paleontologist, taught God is All, and as such God is born in human's cellular structures.

I believe him.

42

Sermon, August 6, 2017

The story of Jesus feeding the 5000 men is found in all four gospels. Today, we read Luke's version. It is a little different from the other three, but basically they all tell a similar story. However, in reading the story we must remember the Bible is about spirituality not physicality. Biblical stories are spiritual stories told to enhance our own spirituality. The stories are not literal. In effect, it doesn't matter if the story is factual. What matters is the meaning of the story. Churches for 2000 years have tried to find a way of explaining the food expansion of two fish and five loaves of bread, even sometimes going so far as to say Jesus was a magician.

These false teachings have lived into the present. I think it is time to look again.

Let me tell you right now this is not a story about food. It is a thematic story that reoccurs all through the Old and New Testaments. Feeding, nurturing, nourishing are primary Biblical themes. The nourishing does not come from cheese and eggs and lamb chops, or from literal bread and fish. It comes, rather, by telling people about God's love, His care for every human, about hope, and the joyous life available through faith.

In early times the fish was a symbol of Jesus and his unfailing faith. Jesus called his disciples fishers of men. We know then, this story is about Jesus himself and his teachings.

Even though Jesus gave fresh meaning to the old Jewish stories, none the less, most of the stories were re-telling of those found in the Torah, the Pentateuch, the five books of Moses. Immediately when we read the crowd was hungry, we know they were hungry for inspiration, hope, love, and acceptance in a time and place where those traits were all but non-existent.

When the disciples said to Jesus the people are hungry they complained that all they had were two fish and five loaves of bread. Jesus told them, "Then you have enough." The two fish were the two identities of Jesus: rabbi meaning teacher and healer. The five loaves of bread were the laws that directed every aspect of Jewish life found in the book of Torah.

Jesus told the disciples to go, break up the crowd into groups of fifty. Then he said to the disciples, "You feed them." The disciples obeyed. Each disciple sat down with a group of fifty. It was their hands-on training in how to teach crowds of people. The disciples must have done a good job because the people were satisfied. Twelve basketfuls of broken pieces were collected. That statement means the twelve disciples were the baskets of nourishment and they were not completely ready for their missionary jobs. They were still-broken pieces. They had more training to receive. But that is a story for another sermon.

This powerful story is not about Jesus as a magician. It is not about literal food expansion. It is not a factual story. Rather it is a lovely, often repeated, theme that all good things come from God. These good things are manifested in humans, shared by humans, and acted on by humans having a relationship with the one who, in our faith tradition, lived the grace of God more than any other: Jesus, the one we call Christ.

43

God — by whatever name we call our Creator — knows what's what.

The God I worship molded me, a self-centered, shy, young mass of confusion wanting to please those around me, and made of me something of worth. I have an inner peace, an innate sense of value, simply because I exist. The breath of God is in me. Therefore I live. There needs to be no reason to exist other than to choose to be one reflection of God-given light to a dark and disappointing world.

What God has made of my life is a powerful lesson: to trust that the worst that can happen to us can also be the best thing to happen. I am no longer afraid of change. I welcome it, for it might lead to transformation. Which, again, is our primary task during this earthly phase of our existence.

I experienced life-altering lessons throughout my years.

I believe I came of age spiritually during my minimalist period when I survived through the largesse of people sometimes unknown to me. Blessings, often called miracles, came to me as gifts from the universe, unasked for and unexpected. With those favors how could I not be certain there is a caring entity beyond myself, which is also a core part of me.

I accept life as complete when it has suffering and hardships intermingled with joy and peace. These characteristics give meaning to each other. Their intermingling is foundational to understanding love must incorporate multi-faceted experiences to force growth, to deny a crippling status quo, and to move beyond self into a broad existence of spiritual connections, empowering us to be more than we are

With every loss I experienced, life provided new opportunities.

My beloved Floy died; my first child was born.

The loss of my mother almost crippled me, but Westminster Academy was birthed and thrived for 45 years.

Neil and I divorced, yet our time in Scotland opened my eyes to a wider, unfolding spirituality, changing my faith in drastic ways.

The divorces from John were debilitating in many ways, but my creativity blossomed. I wrote a small book called *Divorce* and held workshops to help women cope. That was also the time, Dr. Gail Cotton, son Neil, and I established a national magazine for high school and college debaters *Progressive Forensics*.

The loss of trust in Ron's and my relationship and the security it had provided left a gap that was filled by Gertrude Ford and her generosity. Her gift paved the way for my ordination and led to the establishment of The Nourishing Place.

This ministry is like a space nebulae that constantly births new stars to fill the void made by an ever-expanding universe. Our shared worship at the Nourishing Place gives birth to awareness that love and forgiveness are two sides of one matter. This understanding makes possible an ever-expanding spirituality resulting in circles of unconditional love.

What we give returns.

These twenty years as a minister, I've learned amazing things about Gentiles and genitals, sinners and saints, the Bible, worship/preaching/church phenomenon, and most of all, about myself.

I've also come to an understanding that we are all alike — and like it or not, we are all like another phenomenon we call Jesus.

• • •

I have lived primarily during the Twentieth Century and so far seventeen years of the Twenty-first Century. Yet I intimately knew and had contact with my grandparents and older relatives who were born in the mid 1860's. Our great grandchild was born in 2016.

My living memories span over 150 years.

I am awed by the cultural and technical changes that have occurred during that span of years. Yet I am equally amazed by the values that have not changed, such as respect for one another, being kind, doing the best we can, seeking to serve rather than be served. All of these are major teachings of Rabbi Jesus, the intent of which is to lift us up to see that sky and earth are One.

My great-great Uncle Wayne Welborn, from Jones County, Mississippi, lived and farmed at a time when there were no tractors or cars, no electricity, and no indoor plumbing. In spite of the primitiveness of farm equipment, the United States Congress acknowledged his being the most successful agriculturist of his era, as reported in a newspaper article I recently discovered in a box of family mementos. During one of 96-year-old Uncle Wayne's visits to our Camp Avenue home, he teased my grandmother Floy about her childhood. She climbed down the hill to Ten Mile Creek every morning to pick mint leaves. He said she chewed them up to freshen her breath in case neighborhood boys came to call. There were no toothbrushes in rural Mississippi.

Neither were there telephones, radios, televisions, and certainly no iPads or computers — all of which our seven year old grandsons use competently.

I wish I could pick up a telephone to see my grandmother's face. But I can telephone and facetime with *my* grandchildren, though we live miles apart.

For me to live in the midst of this time span between great-great uncles and a great-grandbaby holds some sense of urgency for me. My desire is to remember what I can from my own varied experience and from the oral history of my family and record some of it for my grandchildren.

Perhaps these stories will be passed on to those yet to come. I write this memoir to honor those who lived before me and encourage those who come after me.

EPILOGUE

Westminster Academy, after a successful 45-year run, changed its name to Hope Academy.

Neil Jr. is a retired federal administrative judge. He has been married to Jill Averett White for 40+ years. People still talk about the sermon he gave at Westminster Presbyterian Church in 1969.

I'm not certain as to the whereabouts of my second (and third) husband, **John.**

Stepson Todd works at John C. Space Center in Bay St. Louis and lives in Slidell, Louisiana with his wife and three children.

After retiring as a medicinal chemist, **Ron Borne,** brilliant scientists and Renaissance man took up writing. He published two books — *Beginnings and Ends* and *Troutmouth* — before he died on October 18, 2016. His third book, *Big Nasty: Jim Carmody, Mississippi's Coach* (completed three days before he died) will be published posthumously by Nautilus Publishing in the Fall of 2017. Ron Borne's children: Debra, Mike, and Meribeth are all successful in their chosen fields. I feel close to each one. Grandson Neil White IV has always considered Ron a grandfather.

Max Peck, true to his word, has supported me completely over the last twenty years. I have never taken a salary from The Nourishing Place. Worries about money have never interfered with my work or ministry. Max's son Maxwell Peck III and his wife Donna have three children: Maren, Maxwell IV, and Mason. Though these children are not in my biological gene pool they are definitely part of me…especially my heart.

Cynthia Melvin Hutchinson and husband John have moved from California to South Carolina.

Janice Fant Carpenter lives in Wiggins, MS with her husband Ben

June closed As You Like It after a successful 45 year run. She and David Vincent have been married for thirty-nine years

Tish married and moved to Washington State in 1975.

My son, **Jamie,** graduated at the top of his law school class. After practicing law for 17 years, he now flies helicopters full-time for the Army

National Guard. He lives in Oxford and is married to Heather White. They have two children, Camille and Charlie. Jamie is currently deployed in Kosovo.

My daughter **Liz** has worked in the legal and education fields. She currently teaches kindergarten students in Louisiana. She and her husband Sal live in Ponchatoula, Louisiana. Their daughter Katie is the mother of a one-year-old son, Tyler.

My son, **Harry**, lives in Zurich, Switzerland with his partner Jens. Harry plays classical saxophone with some of the finest orchestras in the world.

My son, **Neil III**, lives in Oxford with his wife Debbie Bell. He operates Nautilus Publishing. In 2009, his memoir, *In the Sanctuary of Outcasts* — about his year in the prison/leprosarium — was published by Harper-Collins. His son, **Neil IV**, is a Ph.D. student at the University of Texas. His daughter, **Maggie**, works for Tulane University and performs improv at night in New Orleans. Debbie's daughter Lindsay and her husband Jake live in New Orleans. They have one daughter, Julia.

Alma Savoy died in 2014 and her daughter Mary died in 2016. Mary's husband Al is an important part of our family.

Gail Cotton died on November 3, 2008. The Nourishing Place wouldn't be here were it not for Gail's dedication and faith.

Jo Kennedy retired as Director of the Cheshire Homes in Gulfport. She prepared breakfast at the Nourishing Place every Sunday from 1997-2004. She now suffers from Post-Polio Syndrome and is homebound (but she has not lost her sense of humor).

Capt. Bob Engram died in 2013. His wife **Carmen**, at age 92, remains our steadfast and faithful family friend.

In August of 2015, we held a funeral for **Hurricane Katrina** on its tenth anniversary at The Nourishing Place. While others were holding remembrances and publishing special editions, we wanted to put that bad girl to rest.

In 1997 when I finally said a resounding, "Yes, I will become an ordained Christian minister!" I looked for **Eula Jones** to tell her about my decision. I discovered she had died in 1993. Her body rests in a country cemetery in the north part of Harrison County.

After **Gertrude (Gayle) Ford** died her estate built the Gertrude Ford Performing Arts Center on the Ole Miss campus. Several other buildings have been built in her honor on college and university campuses around Mississippi

The **Miriam Weems portrait of Harry** (much to the delight of Neil and Jamie) now hangs in a downstairs bathroom at my condo.

Artist **Emmitt Thames** and his wife Linda surprised us in 2015 with a portrait he painted of me without my knowing. The portrait is on the cover of this book.

The Nourishing Place christened its third home on September 10, 2017.

ACKNOWLEDGEMENTS

Thank you to Max for support and encouragement, aways and in all ways. Gratitude to Neil III for long hours of editing, to Liz for typing and retyping this manuscript, and to Harry and Jamie for helping me remember. Thanks to family and friends who enrich my life by sharing yourselves with me. To Mary Ann Reed Bowen for proofreading.

And to our Almighty God for the opportunity to live.